AF447524

RESTORATIVE JUSTICE IN THE BOOK OF PHILEMON

How Apostle Paul Uses Restorative Justice Techniques to Restore Relationship Between Philemon and Onesimus

Dr. Maxwell Shimba

Copyright © 2024 – Dr. Maxwell Shimba

All rights reserved. No portion of this book may be reproduced, stored in a retrieval system, or transmitted in any form or by any means – electronics, mechanical, photocopy, recording, scanning, or other – except for brief quotations in critical reviews or articles, without the prior written permission of the publisher.

Shimba Publishing, LLC.

Printed in the United States of America

TABLE OF CONTENTS

PREFACE

In our modern world, the concept of justice is often synonymous with punishment and retribution. We see it in our legal systems, in our societal norms, and sometimes even in our personal relationships. Yet, for those of us who seek to live by the teachings of Jesus Christ, there is a different path—a path that leads to healing, restoration, and reconciliation. This path is illuminated in the brief yet profoundly impactful letter of Paul to Philemon.

The Book of Philemon is one of the shortest books in the New Testament, but its significance is immense. It is a personal letter from Paul, written during his imprisonment, to a fellow Christian named Philemon. The letter concerns Onesimus, a runaway slave who had wronged Philemon but had since encountered Paul and converted to Christianity. Paul's appeal to Philemon to forgive Onesimus and receive him as a brother in Christ is a powerful example of restorative justice in action.

In this book, we will explore how the principles of restorative justice are not only biblical but also profoundly transformative. By examining the context, content, and implications of Paul's letter, we will uncover timeless lessons that can be applied in our contemporary world. We will delve into the historical and cultural backdrop of the letter, analyze Paul's approach and strategies, and reflect on the broader impact of his intervention on the early Christian community.

The journey through this exploration is guided by several key principles that Paul exemplifies in his letter: empathy, mediation, restitution, and reconciliation. These principles form the foundation of restorative justice, a concept that seeks to repair the harm caused by wrongdoing rather than simply punishing the offender. By focusing on the restoration of relationships and the healing of communities, restorative justice offers a more holistic and compassionate approach to addressing conflict and harm.

The Relevance of Restorative Justice Today

As we navigate through the complexities of modern society, the principles of restorative justice are more relevant than ever. Our criminal justice systems are often overloaded and punitive, leading to cycles of reoffending and social fragmentation. Community conflicts, whether they arise in neighborhoods, workplaces, or online spaces, can leave deep scars and unresolved tensions. Even within our personal relationships, we frequently struggle with forgiveness and reconciliation.

Paul's letter to Philemon provides a blueprint for addressing these challenges. By practicing empathy, we can better understand the experiences and emotions of others, fostering an environment of mutual respect and compassion. Through mediation, we can facilitate open and constructive dialogue, allowing parties to express their perspectives and work toward resolution. Restitution emphasizes the importance of making amends and taking responsibility for one's actions, promoting accountability and trust. Finally, reconciliation focuses on healing and restoring relationships, building stronger and more cohesive communities.

A Call to Action

This book is not just an academic exploration of Paul's letter; it is a call to action. As believers and followers of Christ, we are called to embody the principles of restorative justice in our own lives and communities. This means actively seeking to repair harm, foster understanding, and promote healing wherever we encounter conflict and injustice.

Throughout the chapters of this book, you will find study questions, discussion guides, and practical steps to help you apply the lessons from Philemon in your own context. These tools are designed to facilitate personal reflection, group discussions, and community initiatives, enabling you to engage deeply with the principles of restorative justice and put them into practice.

Gratitude and Hope

I am deeply grateful to all those who have contributed to the writing and publication of this book. Your support, insights, and encouragement have been invaluable. I also extend my heartfelt thanks to the countless individuals and communities who practice restorative justice every day, often in challenging and difficult circumstances. Your commitment to healing and reconciliation is a testament to the enduring power of these principles.

It is my hope that this book will inspire and equip you to embrace restorative justice in your own life. May the lessons from Paul's letter to Philemon guide you in your journey toward healing, reconciliation, and justice. Together, let us work to build a world that reflects the compassion, mercy, and transformative power of Jesus Christ.

Dr. Maxwell Shimba

DR. MAXWELL SHIMBA

CHAPTER 01

INTRODUCTION TO RESTORATIVE JUSTICE

The Concept of Restorative Justice

Restorative justice is a framework for justice that focuses on the rehabilitation of offenders through reconciliation with victims and the community. Unlike retributive justice, which emphasizes punishment, restorative justice seeks to repair the harm caused by criminal behavior. It involves a collaborative process that includes victims, offenders, and community members in finding solutions that promote healing and restoration.

Restorative justice is rooted in the belief that crime causes harm to people and relationships and that justice should focus on repairing that harm. This approach emphasizes accountability, making amends, and, when possible, restoring relationships to a state of health. Key components of restorative justice include:

1. Inclusion of All Stakeholders: Restorative justice brings together all parties affected by a crime – the victim, the offender, and the community – to discuss the impact of the crime and determine how best to repair the harm.

2. Voluntary Participation: Participation in restorative justice processes is voluntary. All parties must agree to participate and have a genuine interest in resolving the conflict and restoring relationships.

3. Focus on Harm and Needs: The primary focus is on the harm caused by the crime and the needs of those affected. This contrasts with traditional justice systems, which focus on what laws were broken and what punishment should be imposed.

4. Accountability and Responsibility: Offenders are encouraged to take responsibility for their actions and to understand the impact of their behavior on others. This accountability is seen as a crucial step towards rehabilitation.

5. Reparation and Reintegration: The goal is to make amends and reintegrate offenders into the community. This might involve apologies, restitution, community service, or other actions that address the harm caused.

Restorative justice is not a new concept. It has roots in many indigenous cultures that emphasized community-based approaches to justice and conflict resolution. These practices were often holistic, focusing on healing and restoring balance within the community rather than simply punishing the offender.

In modern times, restorative justice began to gain recognition in the 1970s and 1980s as an alternative to the punitive approaches that dominated Western legal systems. It has since been implemented in various forms around the world, including victim-offender mediation, restorative circles, and community conferencing.

The goals of restorative justice can be summarized as follows:

1. Repairing Harm: Addressing the needs of victims and the community and helping offenders understand the impact of their actions.

2. Restoring Relationships: Encouraging dialogue and reconciliation between victims, offenders, and community members.

3. Rehabilitating Offenders: Helping offenders to take responsibility, make amends, and reintegrate into society.

4. Strengthening Communities: Building stronger, more cohesive communities that are capable of resolving conflicts and supporting their members.

The Process of Restorative Justice

Restorative justice typically involves a series of steps designed to bring about healing and resolution. These steps include:

1. Referral and Preparation: The process usually begins with a referral from the criminal justice system, schools, or community organizations. Participants are then prepared for the restorative justice meeting through individual sessions where the process is explained, and their concerns and needs are addressed.

2. Facilitated Dialogue: A trained facilitator guides the restorative justice meeting, ensuring that all participants have an opportunity to speak and be heard. The dialogue focuses on the impact of the crime, the harm caused, and the steps needed to make amends.

3. Agreement and Follow-Up: The meeting concludes with an agreement on how the offender will make amends. This agreement is created collaboratively and is designed to meet the needs of the victim and the community while holding the offender accountable. Follow-up meetings may be held to ensure that the agreement is being fulfilled.

Restorative justice offers numerous benefits, including:

1. Empowerment: Victims have a voice in the justice process and can express their needs and feelings directly to the offender.

2. Healing: By addressing the harm caused, restorative justice helps victims and offenders move forward and promotes emotional healing.

3. Accountability: Offenders are encouraged to take responsibility for their actions and understand the impact of their behavior.

4. Reduced Recidivism: Studies have shown that restorative justice can reduce reoffending rates by helping offenders develop empathy and a sense of responsibility.

5. Community Cohesion: Restorative justice strengthens community ties and fosters a sense of collective responsibility for resolving conflicts.

Challenges and Criticisms

While restorative justice has many benefits, it also faces challenges and criticisms. Some of these include:

1. Voluntary Participation: The success of restorative justice relies on the willingness of all parties to participate. In some cases, victims or offenders may be unwilling or unable to engage in the process.

2. Power Imbalances: Ensuring that power imbalances do not affect the process is crucial. Facilitators must be skilled

in managing these dynamics to ensure that all voices are heard and respected.

3. Resource Intensive: Restorative justice can be resource-intensive, requiring trained facilitators and significant time and effort to prepare and conduct meetings.

4. Public Perception: Some critics argue that restorative justice may be perceived as being too lenient on offenders. Balancing the need for accountability with the goals of healing and restoration can be challenging.

Restorative justice offers a powerful alternative to traditional punitive approaches to justice. By focusing on repairing harm, restoring relationships, and rehabilitating offenders, it promotes healing and reconciliation within communities. The principles and practices of restorative justice, as demonstrated in the Book of Philemon, provide valuable insights for contemporary justice systems seeking to address the root causes of crime and promote lasting peace and harmony.

In the following chapters, we will delve deeper into the Book of Philemon, examining how the Apostle Paul utilized restorative justice techniques to mend the relationship between Philemon and Onesimus. We will explore the historical context, analyze the letter in detail, and draw lessons for modern restorative justice practices.

The Concept of Restorative Justice

Restorative justice is a framework for justice that focuses on the rehabilitation of offenders through reconciliation with victims and the community. Unlike retributive justice, which emphasizes punishment, restorative justice seeks to repair the harm caused by criminal behavior. It involves a collaborative process that includes victims, offenders, and community members in finding solutions that promote healing and restoration.

Understanding Restorative Justice

Restorative justice is rooted in the belief that crime causes harm to people and relationships and that justice should focus on repairing that harm. This approach emphasizes accountability, making amends, and, when possible, restoring relationships to a state of health. Key components of restorative justice include:

1. Inclusion of All Stakeholders: Restorative justice brings together all parties affected by a crime – the victim, the offender, and the community – to discuss the impact of the crime and determine how best to repair the harm.

2. Voluntary Participation: Participation in restorative justice processes is voluntary. All parties must agree to participate and have a genuine interest in resolving the conflict and restoring relationships.

3. Focus on Harm and Needs: The primary focus is on the harm caused by the crime and the needs of those affected. This contrasts with traditional justice systems, which focus on what laws were broken and what punishment should be imposed.

4. Accountability and Responsibility: Offenders are encouraged to take responsibility for their actions and to understand the impact of their behavior on others. This accountability is seen as a crucial step towards rehabilitation.

5. Reparation and Reintegration: The goal is to make amends and reintegrate offenders into the community. This might involve apologies, restitution, community service, or other actions that address the harm caused.

Historical Context and Development

Restorative justice is not a new concept. It has roots in many indigenous cultures that emphasized community-based approaches to justice and conflict resolution. These practices were often holistic, focusing on healing and restoring balance within the community rather than simply punishing the offender.

In modern times, restorative justice began to gain recognition in the 1970s and 1980s as an alternative to the punitive approaches that dominated Western legal systems. It has since been implemented in various forms around the world, including victim-offender mediation, restorative circles, and community conferencing.

The Goals of Restorative Justice

The goals of restorative justice can be summarized as follows:

1. Repairing Harm: Addressing the needs of victims and the community and helping offenders understand the impact of their actions.

2. Restoring Relationships: Encouraging dialogue and reconciliation between victims, offenders, and community members.

3. Rehabilitating Offenders: Helping offenders to take responsibility, make amends, and reintegrate into society.

4. Strengthening Communities: Building stronger, more cohesive communities that are capable of resolving conflicts and supporting their members.

The Process of Restorative Justice

Restorative justice typically involves a series of steps designed to bring about healing and resolution. These steps include:

1. Referral and Preparation: The process usually begins with a referral from the criminal justice system, schools, or community organizations. Participants are then prepared for the restorative justice meeting through individual

sessions where the process is explained, and their concerns and needs are addressed.

2. Facilitated Dialogue: A trained facilitator guides the restorative justice meeting, ensuring that all participants have an opportunity to speak and be heard. The dialogue focuses on the impact of the crime, the harm caused, and the steps needed to make amends.

3. Agreement and Follow-Up: The meeting concludes with an agreement on how the offender will make amends. This agreement is created collaboratively and is designed to meet the needs of the victim and the community while holding the offender accountable. Follow-up meetings may be held to ensure that the agreement is being fulfilled.

Benefits of Restorative Justice

Restorative justice offers numerous benefits, including:

1. Empowerment: Victims have a voice in the justice process and can express their needs and feelings directly to the offender.

2. Healing: By addressing the harm caused, restorative justice helps victims and offenders move forward and promotes emotional healing.

3. Accountability: Offenders are encouraged to take responsibility for their actions and understand the impact of their behavior.

4. Reduced Recidivism: Studies have shown that restorative justice can reduce reoffending rates by helping offenders develop empathy and a sense of responsibility.

5. Community Cohesion: Restorative justice strengthens community ties and fosters a sense of collective responsibility for resolving conflicts.

Challenges and Criticisms

While restorative justice has many benefits, it also faces challenges and criticisms. Some of these include:

1. Voluntary Participation: The success of restorative justice relies on the willingness of all parties to participate. In some cases, victims or offenders may be unwilling or unable to engage in the process.

2. Power Imbalances: Ensuring that power imbalances do not affect the process is crucial. Facilitators must be skilled in managing these dynamics to ensure that all voices are heard and respected.

3. Resource Intensive: Restorative justice can be resource-intensive, requiring trained facilitators and significant time and effort to prepare and conduct meetings.

4. Public Perception: Some critics argue that restorative justice may be perceived as being too lenient on offenders. Balancing the need for accountability with the goals of healing and restoration can be challenging.

Restorative justice offers a powerful alternative to traditional punitive approaches to justice. By focusing on repairing harm, restoring relationships, and rehabilitating offenders, it promotes healing and reconciliation within communities. The principles and practices of restorative justice, as demonstrated in the Book of Philemon, provide valuable insights for contemporary justice systems seeking to address the root causes of crime and promote lasting peace and harmony.

In the following chapters, we will delve deeper into the Book of Philemon, examining how the Apostle Paul utilized restorative justice techniques to mend the relationship between Philemon and Onesimus. We will explore the historical context, analyze the letter in detail, and draw lessons for modern restorative justice practices.

Overview of the Book of Philemon

The Book of Philemon is one of the shortest books in the New Testament, yet it carries profound lessons on forgiveness, reconciliation, and restorative justice. Written by the Apostle Paul, this epistle is a personal letter to Philemon, a wealthy Christian in Colossae, regarding Onesimus, a runaway slave who had wronged Philemon but had since become a Christian under Paul's guidance.

Historical and Cultural Context

Understanding the historical and cultural context of the Book of Philemon is crucial for grasping its significance. In the Roman Empire, slavery was a common institution, and slaves were considered property of their masters. A runaway slave, like Onesimus, would face severe punishment if caught. However, the early Christian community, influenced by the teachings of Jesus, was beginning to challenge and redefine social norms, including those related to slavery.

Philemon, the recipient of Paul's letter, was a prominent member of the Christian community in Colossae. He was known for his faith and love for the believers, and his home served as a meeting place for the church. Onesimus, his slave, had fled, potentially stealing from Philemon in the process. During his escape, Onesimus encountered Paul, who was in prison at the time, and under Paul's mentorship, he became a Christian.

The Purpose of Paul's Letter

Paul's letter to Philemon serves multiple purposes. Firstly, it is a personal appeal for Philemon to forgive Onesimus and to receive him not as a slave but as a beloved brother in Christ. Secondly, it seeks to transform the relationship between Philemon and Onesimus from one of master and slave to one of equals in the Christian community. Lastly, the letter provides an early Christian example of restorative justice, emphasizing reconciliation and the healing of relationships over punishment.

Structure and Content of the Letter

The letter to Philemon is structured as follows:

1. Greeting (Verses 1-3): Paul begins with a warm greeting, addressing Philemon, Apphia, Archippus, and the church that meets in Philemon's home. This inclusive greeting sets a communal tone for the letter.

2. Thanksgiving and Prayer (Verses 4-7): Paul expresses gratitude for Philemon's faith and love, highlighting the positive impact he has had on the Christian community. This section builds a foundation of mutual respect and goodwill.

3. The Appeal for Onesimus (Verses 8-21): This is the heart of the letter. Paul makes a heartfelt appeal for Onesimus, acknowledging his past wrongs but emphasizing his transformation and usefulness to both Paul and Philemon. Paul refrains from commanding Philemon, instead appealing to his sense of Christian love and duty.

4. Final Greetings and Benediction (Verses 22-25): Paul concludes the letter with personal greetings from his companions and a benediction, reinforcing the communal bonds among the early Christians.

Key Themes and Messages

The Book of Philemon addresses several key themes and messages:

1. Forgiveness and Reconciliation: Paul urges Philemon to forgive Onesimus and to reconcile with him, highlighting the transformative power of Christian love and forgiveness.

2. Equality in Christ: The letter challenges social norms by advocating for the equal treatment of Onesimus as a brother in Christ, regardless of his status as a slave.

3. Restorative Justice: Paul's approach embodies restorative justice principles, focusing on healing and restoring relationships rather than seeking retribution.

4. Christian Community: The letter underscores the importance of community and mutual support within the Christian faith, emphasizing that personal relationships are integral to the health and growth of the community. Paul's appeal to Philemon highlights the interconnectedness of believers and the collective responsibility to foster reconciliation and unity. By addressing the conflict between

Philemon and Onesimus, Paul not only seeks to restore their relationship but also to strengthen the entire Christian community through the demonstration of forgiveness, acceptance, and love.

The Role of Community in Restorative Justice

Collective Responsibility

Paul's letter illustrates that reconciliation and justice are not solely the responsibilities of the individuals directly involved but are a communal effort. The early Christian community is portrayed as a supportive network that collectively seeks to embody the principles of Christ's teachings. This collective responsibility encourages each member to actively participate in the restoration of relationships and the healing of wounds caused by conflict.

Therefore, although in Christ I could be bold and order you to do what you ought to do, yet I prefer to appeal to you on the basis of love. (Philemon 1:8-9)

Mutual Support

The community's role in supporting both victims and offenders is crucial. Paul's appeal to Philemon to receive Onesimus as a brother reflects the need for mutual support within the Christian community. By fostering an environment where forgiveness and reconciliation are prioritized, the community helps individuals to heal and grow, strengthening the bonds between its members.

So, if you consider me a partner, welcome him as you would welcome me. (Philemon 1:17)

Encouragement for Modern Christian Communities

Building a Supportive Environment

Modern Christian communities can take inspiration from Paul's approach by building environments that support restorative justice principles. This involves creating spaces where open dialogue, empathy, and mutual support are encouraged, allowing members to address conflicts constructively and compassionately.

- Practical Step: Establish small groups or support circles within the church where members can discuss personal conflicts and seek collective guidance and support for reconciliation.

Promoting Education and Awareness

Educating the community about restorative justice and its biblical foundations is essential. By raising awareness and understanding, churches can equip their members with the knowledge and skills needed to practice restorative justice effectively.

- Practical Step: Organize workshops, sermons, and study groups focused on the principles of restorative justice, using Paul's letter to Philemon as a foundational text.

Encouraging Active Participation

Encouraging active participation in restorative practices helps to embed these principles into the fabric of the community. By involving all members in the process of reconciliation, the church can foster a culture of collective responsibility and mutual support.

- Practical Step: Develop church-led initiatives that involve the congregation in restorative justice activities, such as mediation programs, community service projects, and support groups for victims and offenders.

The letter to Philemon serves as a profound reminder of the importance of community and mutual support within the Christian faith. By emphasizing personal relationships and collective responsibility, Paul's approach to restorative justice offers valuable lessons for modern Christian communities. By building supportive environments, promoting education and awareness, and encouraging active participation, contemporary churches can embody the principles of restorative justice, fostering healing, reconciliation, and unity within their communities. Through these efforts, the Christian community can reflect the transformative power of

Christ's love and create a lasting legacy of compassion and justice.

THE CONCEPT OF RESTORATIVE JUSTICE

Restorative justice is a framework for justice that focuses on the rehabilitation of offenders through reconciliation with victims and the community. Unlike retributive justice, which emphasizes punishment, restorative justice seeks to repair the harm caused by criminal behavior. It involves a collaborative process that includes victims, offenders, and community members in finding solutions that promote healing and restoration.

Restorative justice is rooted in the belief that crime causes harm to people and relationships and that justice should focus on repairing that harm. This approach emphasizes accountability, making amends, and, when possible, restoring relationships to a state of health. Key components of restorative justice include:

1. Inclusion of All Stakeholders: Restorative justice brings together all parties affected by a crime – the victim, the offender, and the community – to discuss the impact of the crime and determine how best to repair the harm.

2. Voluntary Participation: Participation in restorative justice processes is voluntary. All parties must agree to

participate and have a genuine interest in resolving the conflict and restoring relationships.

3. Focus on Harm and Needs: The primary focus is on the harm caused by the crime and the needs of those affected. This contrasts with traditional justice systems, which focus on what laws were broken and what punishment should be imposed.

4. Accountability and Responsibility: Offenders are encouraged to take responsibility for their actions and to understand the impact of their behavior on others. This accountability is seen as a crucial step towards rehabilitation.

5. Reparation and Reintegration: The goal is to make amends and reintegrate offenders into the community. This might involve apologies, restitution, community service, or other actions that address the harm caused.

Restorative justice is not a new concept. It has roots in many indigenous cultures that emphasized community-based approaches to justice and conflict resolution. These practices were often holistic, focusing on healing and restoring balance within the community rather than simply punishing the offender.

In modern times, restorative justice began to gain recognition in the 1970s and 1980s as an alternative to the punitive approaches that dominated Western legal systems. It has since been implemented in various forms around the world, including victim-offender mediation, restorative circles, and community conferencing.

The goals of restorative justice can be summarized as follows:

1. Repairing Harm: Addressing the needs of victims and the community and helping offenders understand the impact of their actions.

2. Restoring Relationships: Encouraging dialogue and reconciliation between victims, offenders, and community members.

3. Rehabilitating Offenders: Helping offenders to take responsibility, make amends, and reintegrate into society.

4. Strengthening Communities: Building stronger, more cohesive communities that are capable of resolving conflicts and supporting their members.

Restorative justice typically involves a series of steps designed to bring about healing and resolution. These steps include:

1. Referral and Preparation: The process usually begins with a referral from the criminal justice system, schools, or community organizations. Participants are then prepared for the restorative justice meeting through individual

sessions where the process is explained, and their concerns and needs are addressed.

2. Facilitated Dialogue: A trained facilitator guides the restorative justice meeting, ensuring that all participants have an opportunity to speak and be heard. The dialogue focuses on the impact of the crime, the harm caused, and the steps needed to make amends.

3. Agreement and Follow-Up: The meeting concludes with an agreement on how the offender will make amends. This agreement is created collaboratively and is designed to meet the needs of the victim and the community while holding the offender accountable. Follow-up meetings may be held to ensure that the agreement is being fulfilled.

Restorative justice offers numerous benefits, including:

1. Empowerment: Victims have a voice in the justice process and can express their needs and feelings directly to the offender.

2. Healing: By addressing the harm caused, restorative justice helps victims and offenders move forward and promotes emotional healing.

3. Accountability: Offenders are encouraged to take responsibility for their actions and understand the impact of their behavior.

4. Reduced Recidivism: Studies have shown that restorative justice can reduce reoffending rates by helping offenders develop empathy and a sense of responsibility.

5. Community Cohesion: Restorative justice strengthens community ties and fosters a sense of collective responsibility for resolving conflicts.

Challenges and Criticisms

While restorative justice has many benefits, it also faces challenges and criticisms. Some of these include:

1. Voluntary Participation: The success of restorative justice relies on the willingness of all parties to participate. In some cases, victims or offenders may be unwilling or unable to engage in the process.

2. Power Imbalances: Ensuring that power imbalances do not affect the process is crucial. Facilitators must be skilled in managing these dynamics to ensure that all voices are heard and respected.

3. Resource Intensive: Restorative justice can be resource-intensive, requiring trained facilitators and significant time and effort to prepare and conduct meetings.

4. Public Perception: Some critics argue that restorative justice may be perceived as being too lenient on offenders. Balancing the need for accountability with the goals of healing and restoration can be challenging.

Restorative justice offers a powerful alternative to traditional punitive approaches to justice. By focusing on repairing harm, restoring relationships, and rehabilitating offenders, it promotes healing and reconciliation within communities. The principles and practices of restorative justice, as demonstrated in the Book of Philemon, provide valuable insights for contemporary justice systems seeking to address the root causes of crime and promote lasting peace and harmony.

Overview of the Book of Philemon

The Book of Philemon is one of the shortest books in the New Testament, yet it carries profound lessons on forgiveness, reconciliation, and restorative justice. Written by the Apostle Paul, this epistle is a personal letter to Philemon, a wealthy Christian in Colossae, regarding Onesimus, a runaway slave who had wronged Philemon but had since become a Christian under Paul's guidance.

Historical and Cultural Context

Understanding the historical and cultural context of the Book of Philemon is crucial for grasping its significance. In the Roman Empire, slavery was a common institution, and slaves were considered property of their masters. A runaway slave, like Onesimus, would face severe punishment if caught. However, the early Christian community, influenced by the teachings of Jesus, was beginning to challenge and redefine social norms, including those related to slavery.

Philemon, the recipient of Paul's letter, was a prominent member of the Christian community in Colossae. He was known for his faith and love for the believers, and his home served as a meeting place for the church. Onesimus, his slave, had fled, potentially stealing from Philemon in the process. During his escape, Onesimus encountered Paul, who was in prison at the time, and under Paul's mentorship, he became a Christian.

The Purpose of Paul's Letter

Paul's letter to Philemon serves multiple purposes. Firstly, it is a personal appeal for Philemon to forgive Onesimus and to receive him not as a slave but as a beloved brother in Christ. Secondly, it seeks to transform the relationship between Philemon and Onesimus from one of master and slave to one of equals in the Christian community. Lastly, the letter provides an early Christian example of restorative justice, emphasizing reconciliation and the healing of relationships over punishment.

Structure and Content of the Letter

The letter to Philemon is structured as follows:

1. Greeting (Verses 1-3): Paul begins with a warm greeting, addressing Philemon, Apphia, Archippus, and the

church that meets in Philemon's home. This inclusive greeting sets a communal tone for the letter.

2. Thanksgiving and Prayer (Verses 4-7): Paul expresses gratitude for Philemon's faith and love, highlighting the positive impact he has had on the Christian community. This section builds a foundation of mutual respect and goodwill.

3. The Appeal for Onesimus (Verses 8-21): This is the heart of the letter. Paul makes a heartfelt appeal for Onesimus, acknowledging his past wrongs but emphasizing his transformation and usefulness to both Paul and Philemon. Paul refrains from commanding Philemon, instead appealing to his sense of Christian love and duty.

4. Final Greetings and Benediction (Verses 22-25): Paul concludes the letter with personal greetings from his companions and a benediction, reinforcing the communal bonds among the early Christians.

Key Themes and Messages

The Book of Philemon addresses several key themes and messages:

1. Forgiveness and Reconciliation: Paul urges Philemon to forgive Onesimus and to reconcile with him, highlighting the transformative power of Christian love and forgiveness.

2. Equality in Christ: The letter challenges social norms by advocating for the equal treatment of Onesimus as a brother in Christ, regardless of his status as a slave.

3. Restorative Justice: Paul's approach embodies restorative justice principles, focusing on healing and restoring relationships rather than seeking retribution.

4. Christian Community: The letter underscores the importance of community and mutual support within the Christian faith, emphasizing that personal relationships are integral to spiritual growth and communal harmony.

Purpose and Structure of the Book

This book aims to explore how Paul employs restorative justice techniques in his letter to Philemon to facilitate the reconciliation between Philemon and Onesimus. It will examine the historical context, analyze the letter, and draw lessons for contemporary restorative justice practices.

Purpose of This Book

The purpose of this book is to provide a comprehensive analysis of the Book of Philemon through the lens of restorative justice. By examining Paul's approach to reconciling Philemon and Onesimus, we can uncover valuable insights into early Christian practices of justice and reconciliation. This book seeks to:

1. Explore the Historical Context: Understanding the cultural and historical backdrop of the Roman Empire and the early Christian community will provide deeper insights into the dynamics at play in the letter to Philemon.

2. Analyze Paul's Letter: A detailed examination of the text will reveal the strategies and techniques Paul used to advocate for Onesimus and to encourage Philemon towards forgiveness and reconciliation.

3. Draw Contemporary Lessons: By applying the principles found in the Book of Philemon to modern contexts, we can develop practical applications for restorative justice in today's society.

Structure of This Book

This book is structured into several chapters, each focusing on different aspects of the Book of Philemon and its application to restorative justice:

1. Introduction: An overview of restorative justice, the Book of Philemon, and the purpose and structure of this book.

2. The Context of Philemon: A detailed look at the historical and cultural background of Philemon, Onesimus, and the early Christian community.

3. Restorative Justice in the Early Church: An exploration of early Christian views on justice and

reconciliation, and how these principles are reflected in Paul's writings.

4. The Appeal of Paul: A close analysis of Paul's letter to Philemon, focusing on his tone, approach, and

specific appeal for Onesimus.

5. Key Restorative Justice Techniques Used by Paul: An examination of the restorative justice techniques employed by Paul, including empathy, mediation, reconciliation, and restitution.

6. The Outcome of Paul's Intervention: An assessment of the impact of Paul's letter on Onesimus, Philemon, and the broader early Christian community.

7. Lessons from Philemon for Modern Restorative Justice: Practical applications of the principles found in the Book of Philemon for contemporary restorative justice practices.

8. Conclusion: A summary of key points and the lasting legacy of Paul's approach to restorative justice.

By following this structure, readers will gain a thorough understanding of how the Apostle Paul used restorative justice techniques to facilitate reconciliation between Philemon and Onesimus, and how these principles can be applied in modern contexts to promote healing and restoration.

CHAPTER 02

THE CONTEXT OF PHILEMON

Historical and Cultural Background

In the Roman Empire, slavery was an integral part of the social and economic fabric. Slaves were regarded as the property of their owners and were often subjected to harsh and inhumane treatment. The legal system of the time provided few protections for slaves, and their rights were severely limited. This context is crucial for understanding the dynamics at play in the Book of Philemon.

Slavery in the Roman Empire was pervasive, with slaves making up a significant portion of the population. They were used for a variety of purposes, including manual labor, domestic service, and skilled professions. Slaves could be found in households, farms, mines, and even in administrative roles. The conditions and treatment of slaves varied widely depending on their roles and their owners' dispositions.

Legally, slaves were considered the property of their masters, who had the right to control every aspect of their lives. Masters could buy, sell, punish, and even kill their slaves without facing legal repercussions. Slaves had no legal personhood and could not own property, marry legally, or enter into contracts. Any personal achievements or possessions of a slave were legally attributed to their master.

Runaway slaves were particularly vulnerable. If captured, they faced severe punishments, including flogging, branding, or even execution. The fear of harsh retribution was intended to deter other slaves from attempting to escape.

The Early Christian Community

The early Christian community was a diverse and growing movement within the Roman Empire. Christianity began as a small Jewish sect but quickly spread to Gentiles across the empire. The teachings of Jesus and the apostles emphasized love, forgiveness, and equality, which contrasted sharply with the societal norms of the time, including the institution of slavery.

Social and Religious Dynamics

Early Christians met in homes and formed close-knit communities that transcended traditional social boundaries.

The teachings of Christianity promoted the idea of spiritual equality among believers, regardless of their social status. Passages like Galatians 3:28, which states, "There is neither Jew nor Greek, slave nor free, male nor female, for you are all one in Christ Jesus," were revolutionary in their social implications.

However, while the early church promoted spiritual equality, it did not directly challenge the institution of slavery. Instead, it sought to transform relationships within the existing social framework. This approach is evident in Paul's letters, where he addresses both slaves and masters, urging them to treat each other with Christian love and respect.

Philemon and Onesimus

Philemon was a wealthy Christian convert and a prominent member of the church in Colossae. He was known for his faith and generosity, and his home served as a meeting place for the local Christian community. As a slave owner, Philemon had legal authority over his slaves, including Onesimus.

Onesimus was one of Philemon's slaves who had run away, possibly after committing some wrongdoing. In Roman society, a runaway slave like Onesimus would face severe punishment if caught. However, during his flight, Onesimus encountered the Apostle Paul, who was imprisoned at the time.

The Encounter with Paul

Paul, who referred to himself as a "prisoner of Christ Jesus," was under house arrest but remained active in his ministry. Onesimus found refuge with Paul and converted to Christianity under his mentorship. This conversion was significant, as it transformed Onesimus's identity from a runaway slave to a beloved brother in Christ.

Paul saw great potential in Onesimus and recognized the need to reconcile him with Philemon. He decided to write a personal and heartfelt letter to Philemon, appealing for forgiveness and reconciliation. Paul's letter is an exemplary model of restorative justice, aimed at healing the fractured relationship between Philemon and Onesimus.

The relationship between Philemon and Onesimus was initially one of master and slave, characterized by the legal and social norms of the Roman Empire. Philemon had the authority to punish Onesimus for running away, and the expectation would be severe retribution. However, the introduction of Christian principles into their relationship added a new dimension.

Philemon's Faith and Leadership

Philemon's conversion to Christianity and his role as a leader in the Colossian church are essential to understanding his potential response to Paul's appeal. As a Christian, Philemon was called to live out the teachings of Jesus, which included forgiveness, love, and reconciliation. Paul's letter to Philemon appealed to these values, urging him to act not just as a master but as a fellow believer in Christ.

Onesimus's transformation from a runaway slave to a Christian brother was a radical change. Under Paul's guidance, he became a valued member of the Christian community. Paul's letter describes Onesimus as "my child" and "my very heart," indicating a deep and personal bond. Paul's advocacy for Onesimus is a profound example of restorative justice, emphasizing personal transformation and the restoration of relationships.

Paul's Role as Mediator

Paul's role as a mediator is central to the story. He leveraged his authority and relationship with both Philemon and Onesimus to facilitate reconciliation. Paul's approach was not to command Philemon but to appeal to his sense of Christian duty and love. By offering to repay any debt Onesimus owed and requesting that Philemon welcome Onesimus as he would welcome Paul himself, Paul set a powerful example of restorative justice.

The early church's approach to justice and reconciliation was deeply influenced by the teachings of Jesus and the apostles. The emphasis on love, forgiveness, and community support provided a framework for addressing conflicts and restoring relationships.

Justice in early Christianity was not about retribution but about restoring relationships and healing communities. The teachings of Jesus emphasized forgiveness and reconciliation, urging believers to go beyond the letter of the law and embody the spirit of love and compassion.

Examples from the New Testament

Several New Testament passages illustrate the early church's approach to justice and reconciliation. Jesus' parables, such as the Prodigal Son (Luke 15:11-32), emphasize forgiveness and the joy of reconciliation. Similarly, the teachings of Paul in his letters to various churches stress the importance of love, unity, and mutual support.

Theological Foundations

The theological foundations of early Christian justice are rooted in the belief that all people are made in the image of God and are equal in Christ. This belief challenged social norms and called for a new way of relating to one another, based on mutual respect and love.

Paul's Theology of Reconciliation

Paul's theology of reconciliation is evident in his letters. He consistently urged believers to forgive one another, to seek reconciliation, and to live in harmony. Paul's letter to Philemon is a practical application of these principles, demonstrating how restorative justice can be achieved through personal appeal and mutual respect.

The historical and cultural context of the Book of Philemon provides a rich backdrop for understanding the dynamics of slavery, early Christianity, and restorative justice. By examining the relationship between Philemon and Onesimus and the role of Paul as a mediator, we gain valuable insights into the transformative power of forgiveness and reconciliation.

In the next chapter, we will delve deeper into the early church's views on justice and reconciliation, exploring how these principles are reflected in the New Testament and how they can inform contemporary restorative justice practices. Through a detailed analysis of Paul's letter to Philemon, we will uncover the strategies and techniques he used to advocate for Onesimus and to encourage Philemon towards forgiveness and reconciliation.

THE RELATIONSHIP BETWEEN PHILEMON AND ONESIMUS

The Master-Slave Relationship

The Nature of Slavery in the Roman Empire

In the Roman Empire, the master-slave relationship was a deeply entrenched societal norm. Slaves were regarded as property rather than persons, and their rights were severely restricted. This legal framework allowed masters to exert considerable control over their slaves' lives, including the right to punish them harshly for any disobedience or attempt to escape. Philemon, as a master, held significant power over Onesimus, his slave.

Philemon's Role and Status

Philemon was a wealthy and respected member of the Christian community in Colossae. His home served as a meeting place for the local church, and he was known for his faith and generosity. As a slave owner, Philemon's relationship with Onesimus was governed by the norms and expectations of Roman society, where a master's authority over his slaves was absolute.

Onesimus's Departure

Onesimus's decision to flee from Philemon was a serious transgression in the context of Roman law. Runaway slaves were subject to severe punishment, and their escape was considered both a breach of trust and a challenge to the social order. It is suggested that Onesimus might have stolen from Philemon to support his flight, further complicating the situation.

Paul's Intervention

Onesimus's Conversion

During his escape, Onesimus encountered the Apostle Paul, who was under house arrest. Under Paul's mentorship, Onesimus converted to Christianity. This conversion was transformative, not just spiritually but also socially, as it redefined Onesimus's identity within the Christian community.

Paul's Decision to Mediate

Recognizing the potential for reconciliation, Paul decided to intervene. He wrote a letter to Philemon, appealing for forgiveness and a redefinition of Onesimus's status from a slave to a brother in Christ. Paul's decision to mediate was driven by his commitment to the principles of Christian love and reconciliation.

The Content of Paul's Letter

Greetings and Commendation

Paul begins his letter with a warm greeting to Philemon, Apphia, Archippus, and the church that meets in Philemon's home. This inclusive address sets a communal tone and underscores the collective nature of the Christian faith. Paul commends Philemon for his faith and love, highlighting the positive impact he has had on the Christian community. This commendation builds a foundation of mutual respect and goodwill.

The Appeal for Onesimus

A Heartfelt Plea

The core of Paul's letter is a heartfelt plea for Onesimus. Paul acknowledges Onesimus's past wrongs but emphasizes his transformation and newfound usefulness to both Paul and Philemon. He describes Onesimus as "my child" and "my very heart," indicating a deep and personal bond. This language is intended to evoke empathy and compassion from Philemon.

Transforming the Relationship

Paul's appeal is revolutionary in its implications. He asks Philemon to receive Onesimus not as a slave but as a beloved brother in Christ. This request challenges the social norms of the time and calls for a radical redefinition of their relationship. Paul emphasizes that Onesimus is now "more than a slave," but "a beloved brother."

Offering Restitution

To further support his appeal, Paul offers to repay any debt Onesimus owes to Philemon. This offer of restitution underscores Paul's commitment to justice and reconciliation. By taking responsibility for Onesimus's debt, Paul seeks to remove any financial barrier to Philemon's forgiveness and to demonstrate the sincerity of his plea.

Final Greetings and Benediction

Paul concludes his letter with personal greetings from his companions and a benediction. This section reinforces the communal bonds among the early Christians and emphasizes the interconnectedness of the Christian community. It also serves to remind Philemon that the appeal is supported by the broader Christian fellowship.

The Transformative Power of Paul's Appeal

Redefining Social Norms

Paul's letter to Philemon is a profound example of how Christian principles can challenge and transform social norms. By advocating for Onesimus's acceptance as a brother, Paul redefines the master-slave relationship in a way that promotes equality and mutual respect within the Christian community.

The Role of Forgiveness

Forgiveness is central to Paul's appeal. He urges Philemon to forgive Onesimus, not just for the sake of personal reconciliation but as an expression of Christian love and faith. This emphasis on forgiveness aligns with the teachings of Jesus and the early church, which stressed the importance of forgiving others as a reflection of God's forgiveness.

Restorative Justice in Action

Paul's approach embodies the principles of restorative justice. He seeks to repair the harm caused by Onesimus's actions, restore the relationship between Philemon and Onesimus, and reintegrate Onesimus into the community. This process is characterized by empathy, accountability, and a focus on healing rather than punishment.

Implications for the Early Christian Community

A Model for Conflict Resolution

Paul's letter to Philemon provides a model for conflict resolution within the early Christian community. It demonstrates how issues of wrongdoing and interpersonal conflict can be addressed through dialogue, empathy, and a commitment to reconciliation. This model emphasizes the importance of maintaining unity and harmony within the church.

Promoting Equality and Brotherhood

The redefinition of Onesimus's status as a brother in Christ has broader implications for the early Christian community. It promotes the idea of spiritual equality among believers, regardless of their social status. This principle of equality is foundational to the Christian faith and serves to strengthen the bonds of the community.

The Role of Leaders in Mediating Conflicts

Paul's intervention highlights the role of church leaders in mediating conflicts and promoting reconciliation. As an apostle, Paul leverages his authority and relationships to facilitate a just and compassionate resolution. This example underscores the responsibility of leaders to uphold the principles of justice and love within the community.

The relationship between Philemon and Onesimus, as mediated by Paul, provides a rich case study in the application of restorative justice principles within the early Christian community. By transforming a master-slave relationship into one of brotherhood, Paul's letter challenges social norms and exemplifies the transformative power of Christian love and reconciliation.

In the next chapter, we will explore the broader context of restorative justice in the early church. We will examine how the principles of justice and reconciliation were understood and practiced by the early Christians and how these principles are reflected in the New Testament. This exploration will provide a deeper understanding of the theological foundations of restorative justice and its application in contemporary contexts.

THE ROLE OF APOSTLE PAUL

Paul as a Mediator

The role of the Apostle Paul in the reconciliation between Philemon and Onesimus is central to understanding the transformative power of restorative justice within the early Christian community. Paul, a respected apostle and a spiritual father to both Philemon and Onesimus, takes on the role of a mediator, guiding both parties toward reconciliation with an appeal grounded in love and mutual respect.

Paul's Background and Authority

Paul, formerly known as Saul of Tarsus, was a Pharisee and a persecutor of Christians before his dramatic conversion on the road to Damascus. Following his conversion, Paul became one of the most influential apostles, spreading the message of Christianity throughout the Roman Empire. His extensive missionary journeys, theological insights, and numerous epistles to early Christian communities established him as a central figure in the early church.

Paul's authority as an apostle was widely recognized. He had founded several churches and maintained strong relationships with many Christian communities. His letters, which form a significant portion of the New Testament, addressed various doctrinal, ethical, and practical issues faced by these communities. Despite his authoritative position, Paul often chose to lead through persuasion and personal appeal rather than through commands, reflecting his deep commitment to the principles of love and mutual respect.

Paul's Relationship with Philemon

Philemon was a wealthy Christian and a leader in the Colossian church. His home served as a meeting place for the local Christian community, indicating his prominent role in the church. Paul and Philemon shared a bond of Christian fellowship, strengthened by Philemon's faith and love for the believers. Paul begins his letter by acknowledging Philemon's contributions to the church and expressing gratitude for his faithfulness.

By addressing Philemon as a "dear friend and fellow worker" (Philemon 1:1), Paul sets a tone of mutual respect and camaraderie. He refrains from leveraging his apostolic authority to command Philemon; instead, he chooses to appeal to Philemon's sense of Christian duty and love. This approach underscores Paul's belief in voluntary, heartfelt actions over coerced obedience.

Paul's Relationship with Onesimus

Onesimus was a runaway slave who had wronged Philemon, his master. During his escape, Onesimus encountered Paul, who was under house arrest at the time. Under Paul's mentorship, Onesimus converted to Christianity. This conversion marked a significant transformation in Onesimus's life, as he went from being a fugitive slave to a beloved brother in Christ.

Paul's relationship with Onesimus was deeply personal. He describes Onesimus as "my son, whom I have begotten in my chains" (Philemon 1:10), highlighting the spiritual fatherhood he assumed over Onesimus. Paul's affection for Onesimus is evident as he refers to him as "my very heart" (Philemon 1:12). This intimate bond between Paul and Onesimus adds weight to Paul's appeal for reconciliation.

Paul's Appeal to Philemon

A Heartfelt Plea

Paul's letter to Philemon is a masterful example of a heartfelt plea for reconciliation. Rather than issuing a directive, Paul appeals to Philemon's Christian virtues of love, faith, and forgiveness. He writes, "Therefore, though I might be very bold in Christ to command you what is fitting, yet for love's sake I rather appeal to you" (Philemon 1:8-9). This appeal to love rather than authority is a key aspect of Paul's approach.

Emphasizing Onesimus's Transformation

Paul emphasizes the profound transformation that Onesimus has undergone since his conversion. He acknowledges Onesimus's past failures but focuses on his new identity in Christ. Paul writes, "Formerly he was useless to you, but now he has become useful both to you and to me" (Philemon 1:11). By highlighting Onesimus's newfound usefulness and value, Paul seeks to shift Philemon's perception of Onesimus from a runaway slave to a valuable member of the Christian community.

Offering Restitution

To facilitate reconciliation, Paul offers to make restitution for any wrongs Onesimus may have committed. He writes, "If he has wronged you or owes you anything, charge it to me. I, Paul, am writing this with my own hand: I will pay it back" (Philemon 1:18-19). This offer demonstrates Paul's commitment to justice and his willingness to bear the cost of reconciliation. It also removes any financial barrier that might hinder Philemon's forgiveness of Onesimus.

The Role of Love and Mutual Respect

Paul's appeal to Philemon is grounded in the principles of love and mutual respect. He seeks to create a space where both Philemon and Onesimus can engage in a process of reconciliation based on Christian love. Paul's approach reflects the teachings of Jesus, who emphasized love, forgiveness, and the restoration of relationships.

By addressing Philemon with respect and acknowledging his faith and love, Paul creates an atmosphere conducive to reconciliation. He appeals to Philemon's sense of Christian duty, writing, "I do wish, brother, that I may have some benefit from you in the Lord; refresh my heart in Christ" (Philemon 1:20). This appeal to mutual benefit and refreshment underscores the interconnectedness of the Christian community and the importance of supporting one another in faith.

Theological Implications of Paul's Mediation

Equality in Christ

One of the central theological implications of Paul's mediation is the concept of equality in Christ. By urging Philemon to receive Onesimus as a beloved brother rather than a slave, Paul challenges the social norms of the time. He writes, "No longer as a slave, but better than a slave, as a dear brother" (Philemon 1:16). This redefinition of relationships within the Christian community reflects the radical equality that the gospel proclaims.

Forgiveness and Reconciliation

Paul's appeal emphasizes the importance of forgiveness and reconciliation in the Christian life. He encourages Philemon to forgive Onesimus and to embrace him as a fellow believer. This emphasis on forgiveness aligns with the teachings of Jesus, who instructed his followers to forgive others as they have been forgiven by God (Matthew 6:14-15). Reconciliation, as demonstrated in Paul's letter, is not just a personal act but a communal one that strengthens the bonds within the Christian community.

Paul's approach embodies the principles of restorative justice. He focuses on healing the relationship between Philemon and Onesimus, rather than seeking retribution for Onesimus's wrongs. By advocating for restitution and offering to repay any debt, Paul seeks to address the harm caused and facilitate a process of restoration. This approach reflects the heart of restorative justice, which aims to repair relationships and promote healing within the community.

Apostle Paul's role as a mediator between Philemon and Onesimus provides a powerful example of how restorative justice can be applied within the framework of Christian relationships. Paul's appeal, grounded in love and mutual respect, challenges social norms and promotes reconciliation based on the transformative power of the gospel.

By examining Paul's approach, we gain valuable insights into the principles of restorative justice and their application in the early Christian community. Paul's mediation highlights the importance of empathy, forgiveness, and the redefinition of relationships within the body of Christ. These principles continue to resonate today, offering a model for addressing conflicts and promoting reconciliation in contemporary contexts.

In the next chapter, we will explore the broader context of restorative justice in the early church. We will examine how the principles of justice and reconciliation were understood and practiced by the early Christians and how these principles are reflected in the New Testament. This exploration will provide a deeper understanding of the theological foundations of restorative justice and its application in modern contexts.

CHAPTER 03

RESTORATIVE JUSTICE IN THE EARLY CHURCH

Early Christian Views on Justice and Reconciliation

The early Christian community placed a high value on forgiveness, reconciliation, and communal harmony. These principles were deeply embedded in the teachings of Jesus and the apostles, forming the foundation of the early church's approach to justice. Unlike the prevailing legal systems of the time, which often emphasized retribution and punishment, early Christians viewed justice as a means to restore relationships and maintain community wholeness.

The Teachings of Jesus on Forgiveness and Reconciliation

Jesus' teachings profoundly shaped the early Christian understanding of justice. Central to His message was the call to love one's neighbor, forgive those who wrong us, and seek reconciliation with others.

The Sermon on the Mount

In the Sermon on the Mount, Jesus presented a radical vision of righteousness that went beyond mere legalistic adherence to the law. He taught His followers to turn the other cheek, love their enemies, and pray for those who persecuted them (Matthew 5:38-48). This call to non-retaliation and proactive love laid the groundwork for a restorative approach to justice.

The Parable of the Unforgiving Servant

The parable of the unforgiving servant (Matthew 18:21-35) further illustrates the importance of forgiveness. In this parable, a servant who is forgiven a massive debt by his master refuses to forgive a fellow servant a much smaller debt. The master, upon hearing this, rebukes the unforgiving servant and reinstates his debt. Jesus uses this parable to teach that God's forgiveness towards us should inspire us to forgive others. The parable emphasizes that withholding forgiveness disrupts the flow of grace and reconciliation within the community.

The Parable of the Prodigal Son

The parable of the prodigal son (Luke 15:11-32) is another powerful example of restorative justice in Jesus' teachings. In this story, a father forgives his wayward son and restores him to his place in the family. This act of forgiveness and restoration, despite the son's transgressions, exemplifies the heart of restorative justice — the desire to mend broken relationships and reintegrate individuals into the community.

The Apostolic Teachings on Justice and Reconciliation

The apostles, following Jesus' example, continued to emphasize the importance of forgiveness, reconciliation, and communal harmony in their teachings. Their letters to the early Christian communities are filled with exhortations to live in peace, forgive one another, and maintain unity.

Paul's Theology of Reconciliation

Apostle Paul's writings provide a rich theological foundation for understanding justice and reconciliation in the early church. Paul consistently emphasized that reconciliation with God and with one another is at the heart of the Christian message.

Reconciliation with God

Paul taught that through Christ's death and resurrection, believers are reconciled to God. In 2 Corinthians 5:18-19, Paul writes, "All this is from God, who reconciled us to himself through Christ and gave us the ministry of reconciliation: that God was reconciling the world to himself in Christ, not counting people's sins against them." This reconciliation with God is the basis for the call to reconcile with others.

Paul also stressed the importance of reconciliation within the Christian community. In Ephesians 4:32, he exhorts believers to "be kind and compassionate to one another, forgiving each other, just as in Christ God forgave you." This call to forgiveness and kindness reflects the restorative approach to justice, where the focus is on healing and restoring relationships.

For Paul, love is the supreme virtue that binds the community together. In Colossians 3:14, he writes, "And over all these virtues put on love, which binds them all together in perfect unity." Love, according to Paul, is the foundation for all interactions within the Christian community, including the pursuit of justice and reconciliation.

Examples of Restorative Justice in the New Testament

The New Testament provides several examples of restorative justice in action, demonstrating how the early Christians applied these principles in their communal life.

The Jerusalem Council

The Jerusalem Council (Acts 15) is an early example of the church addressing a conflict through a process that aimed at reconciliation and unity. The council was convened to address the contentious issue of whether Gentile converts to Christianity needed to observe Jewish law. Through open dialogue and mutual respect, the council reached a decision that promoted unity and inclusivity, exemplifying a restorative approach to resolving conflicts.

The Case of Onesimus and Philemon

As discussed in the previous chapters, the case of Onesimus and Philemon is a poignant example of restorative justice. Paul's appeal for Onesimus, a runaway slave, to be received back by Philemon as a brother in Christ, emphasizes forgiveness, restoration, and the redefinition of relationships based on the transformative power of the gospel.

The Reconciliation of Peter and Paul

Another significant example is the reconciliation between Peter and Paul. Despite their differences and conflicts, particularly regarding the inclusion of Gentiles in the Christian community (Galatians 2:11-14), they worked towards reconciliation and mutual respect. This example highlights the importance of resolving conflicts and maintaining unity within the leadership of the early church.

The Early Church's Practice of Restorative Justice

Communal Living and Mutual Support

The early Christians practiced a form of communal living that embodied restorative justice principles. Acts 2:44-47 describes how believers "had everything in common," sold the property to provide for those in need, and shared meals with glad and sincere hearts. This practice of mutual support and generosity reflects a commitment to community wholeness and the restoration of relationships.

Church Discipline and Restoration

The early church also dealt with issues of sin and discipline in a restorative manner. For example, in 1 Corinthians 5, Paul addresses a case of immorality within the church. While he calls for the offender to be removed from the community to prevent further harm, his ultimate goal is the offender's repentance and restoration. In 2 Corinthians 2:6-8, Paul urges the church to forgive and comfort the repentant offender, reaffirming their love and restoring him to the community.

The Role of Elders and Leaders

Church leaders, such as elders, played a crucial role in promoting restorative justice. They were responsible for guiding the community, resolving conflicts, and ensuring that justice was administered with compassion and fairness. The qualifications for elders, as outlined in 1 Timothy 3 and Titus 1, emphasize qualities such as being temperate, respectable, hospitable, and able to manage their households well, all of which are essential for fostering a restorative justice environment.

Theological Foundations of Restorative Justice

The Image of God

The theological foundation of restorative justice in the early church is rooted in the belief that all people are made in the image of God (Genesis 1:27). This belief affirms the inherent dignity and worth of every individual, regardless of their status or actions. It calls for a justice that seeks to restore and honor that dignity.

The New Creation in Christ

Another key theological foundation is the concept of the new creation in Christ. Paul writes in 2 Corinthians 5:17, "Therefore, if anyone is in Christ, the new creation has come: The old has gone, the new is here!" This new identity in Christ calls for transformed relationships and communities, where justice is pursued through reconciliation and restoration rather than retribution.

The Ministry of Reconciliation

The ministry of reconciliation, as described by Paul in 2 Corinthians 5:18-19, is central to the mission of the church. Believers are called to be ambassadors of Christ, promoting reconciliation in their relationships and communities. This ministry reflects the heart of restorative justice, which seeks to heal and restore broken relationships.

The early Christian views on justice and reconciliation, as shaped by the teachings of Jesus and the apostles, provide a rich foundation for understanding restorative justice. By emphasizing forgiveness, reconciliation, and communal harmony, the early church offered a radical alternative to the retributive justice systems of their time. Through their teachings and practices, they demonstrated that true justice is about restoring relationships and maintaining community wholeness.

In the next chapter, we will delve into the detailed analysis of Paul's letter to Philemon, exploring how he employed restorative justice techniques to facilitate the reconciliation between Philemon and Onesimus. We will examine the specific strategies Paul used and draw lessons for contemporary restorative justice practices.

EXAMPLES OF RESTORATIVE JUSTICE IN THE NEW TESTAMENT

Instances of restorative justice are prominent in the New Testament, reflected in the teachings and interactions of Jesus and the apostles. These examples illustrate the early Christian commitment to forgiveness, reconciliation, and the restoration of relationships. By examining these instances, we gain a deeper understanding of how restorative justice was practiced and its transformative impact on individuals and communities.

The Forgiveness of the Adulterous Woman (John 8:1-11)

Context and Background

The story of the adulterous woman in John 8:1-11 is a powerful example of Jesus' approach to justice and forgiveness. The narrative begins with the scribes and Pharisees bringing a woman caught in adultery to Jesus. According to the Law of Moses, such an act warranted stoning. However, their true intent was to trap Jesus, hoping to find grounds to accuse Him.

Jesus' Response

Instead of responding immediately, Jesus stoops down and writes on the ground with His finger. When pressed for an answer, He famously replies, "Let any one of you who is without sin be the first to throw a stone at her" (John 8:7). This response shifts the focus from the woman's guilt to the accusers' self-righteousness and sinfulness. Convicted by their consciences, the accusers gradually leave, beginning with the eldest.

Once alone with the woman, Jesus asks, "Woman, where are they? Has no one condemned you?" When she replies that no one has, Jesus declares, "Then neither do I condemn you. Go now and leave your life of sin" (John 8:10-11). Jesus' response exemplifies restorative justice in several ways:

1. Compassion and Empathy: Jesus shows compassion for the woman, addressing her not as a sinner but as a person deserving of dignity and respect.

2. Accountability without Condemnation: Jesus acknowledges the woman's sin but chooses not to condemn her. Instead, He calls her to repentance and a transformed life.

3. Restoration of Dignity: By dismissing the crowd and speaking directly to the woman, Jesus restores her dignity and offers her a chance for a new beginning.

The Parable of the Prodigal Son (Luke 15:11-32)

Context and Background

The parable of the prodigal son, found in Luke 15:11-32, is one of Jesus' most well-known teachings on forgiveness and reconciliation. The parable tells the story of a father and his two sons. The younger son demands his share of the inheritance, leaves home, and squanders his wealth in reckless living. When a famine strikes, he finds himself destitute and decides to return to his father, hoping to be accepted as a hired servant.

The Father's Response

Upon seeing his son returning, the father runs to him, embraces him, and orders a celebration, declaring, "For this son of mine was dead and is alive again; he was lost and is found" (Luke 15:24). This response is remarkable given the cultural context, where the son's actions would have brought significant shame and dishonor to the family.

The parable highlights several key aspects of restorative justice:

1. Unconditional Forgiveness: The father's immediate and unconditional forgiveness demonstrates a deep commitment to restoring the relationship with his son, irrespective of the son's past actions.

2. Reconciliation and Celebration: The father's decision to celebrate the son's return reflects the joy of reconciliation and the restoration of the son's place in the family.

3. Restoring Relationships: The father's actions not only restore the son's status but also aim to heal the fractured family dynamics, including the elder son's resentment.

The Healing of the Paralytic (Mark 2:1-12)

Context and Background

In Mark 2:1-12, Jesus heals a paralyzed man brought to Him by four friends. Unable to reach Jesus due to the crowds, the friends lower the man through the roof of the house where Jesus is teaching. Jesus, seeing their faith, tells the paralytic, "Son, your sins are forgiven" (Mark 2:5).

The Reaction and Jesus' Response

The scribes present question Jesus' authority to forgive sins, considering it blasphemy. In response, Jesus asks, "Which is easier: to say to this paralyzed man, 'Your sins are forgiven,' or to say, 'Get up, take your mat and walk'?" (Mark 2:9). He then heals the man, demonstrating His authority to forgive sins.

This miracle highlights several restorative justice principles:

1. Holistic Healing: Jesus addresses both the physical and spiritual needs of the paralytic, emphasizing that true restoration involves healing the whole person.

2. Community Involvement: The faith and actions of the paralytic's friends play a crucial role in his healing, illustrating the importance of community support in the restorative process.

3. Authority to Forgive: Jesus' authority to forgive sins underscores the restorative nature of His mission, offering

individuals a chance for renewed relationships with God and others.

The Conversion of Zacchaeus (Luke 19:1-10)

Context and Background

Zacchaeus, a chief tax collector in Jericho, is described as wealthy but despised by his fellow Jews for collaborating with the Roman authorities and extorting money. Hearing that Jesus is passing through, Zacchaeus climbs a sycamore tree to see Him. Jesus calls him down and declares His intention to stay at Zacchaeus' house.

Moved by Jesus' acceptance, Zacchaeus makes a public declaration: "Look, Lord! Here and now I give half of my possessions to the poor, and if I have cheated anybody out of anything, I will pay back four times the amount" (Luke 19:8). Jesus responds, "Today salvation has come to this house, because this man, too, is a son of Abraham" (Luke 19:9).

The story of Zacchaeus illustrates restorative justice in several ways:

1. Invitation and Acceptance: Jesus' willingness to engage with Zacchaeus despite his social status demonstrates an inclusive approach that values every individual.

2. Repentance and Restitution: Zacchaeus' commitment to repay those he has wronged reflects genuine

repentance and the importance of making amends as part of the restorative process.

3. Restored Identity: Jesus' declaration that Zacchaeus is a "son of Abraham" restores his identity and place within the community, emphasizing the transformative power of reconciliation.

The Reconciliation of Peter and Jesus (John 21:15-19)

Context and Background

After Jesus' resurrection, He appears to His disciples by the Sea of Galilee. During a meal, Jesus addresses Peter, who had denied Him three times before the crucifixion. Jesus asks Peter three times, "Do you love me?" Each time, Peter affirms his love, and Jesus instructs him to "feed my sheep" (John 21:17).

This interaction between Jesus and Peter exemplifies restorative justice through:

1. Reaffirming Commitment: By asking Peter to affirm his love three times, Jesus gives Peter the opportunity to atone for his three denials, symbolically restoring his commitment.

2. Recommissioning: Jesus' instructions to "feed my sheep" reinstate Peter's role and responsibility within the early church, emphasizing trust and reconciliation.

3. Personal Restoration: This conversation not only restores Peter's relationship with Jesus but also heals his sense

of failure and guilt, enabling him to move forward in his mission.

The New Testament is rich with examples of restorative justice, demonstrating how Jesus and the early Christians prioritized forgiveness, reconciliation, and the restoration of relationships. These instances illustrate the transformative power of restorative justice, not only in addressing individual wrongs but also in fostering communal harmony and wholeness.

By examining these examples, we gain valuable insights into the principles and practices of restorative justice that can inform contemporary efforts to resolve conflicts and heal relationships. In the next chapter, we will conduct a detailed analysis of Paul's letter to Philemon, exploring the specific strategies he used to facilitate reconciliation between Philemon and Onesimus and drawing lessons for modern restorative justice practices.

PAUL'S THEOLOGY OF RECONCILIATION

Paul's writings often emphasize the importance of reconciliation, both with God and among believers. His theology underscores the transformative power of the gospel in restoring broken relationships. Through his letters, Paul provides a comprehensive framework for understanding reconciliation as a central element of the Christian faith.

The Foundation of Reconciliation in Paul's Theology

Reconciliation with God

At the heart of Paul's theology is the concept of reconciliation with God through Jesus Christ. Paul believed that humanity's relationship with God was fundamentally broken due to sin. However, through the sacrificial death and resurrection of Jesus, this relationship could be restored.

The Doctrine of Justification

Paul's doctrine of justification by faith is closely linked to the idea of reconciliation. In his letter to the Romans, Paul writes, "Therefore, since we have been justified through faith, we have peace with God through our Lord Jesus Christ" (Romans 5:1). Justification refers to the act of being declared righteous before God, which is made possible through faith in Jesus Christ. This justification leads to peace with God, marking the beginning of reconciliation.

The Ministry of Reconciliation

In 2 Corinthians 5:18-19, Paul articulates the ministry of reconciliation: "All this is from God, who reconciled us to himself through Christ and gave us the ministry of reconciliation: that God was reconciling the world to himself in Christ, not counting people's sins against them." This passage highlights two key points:

1. Divine Initiative: Reconciliation is initiated by God, who takes the first step in mending the broken relationship with humanity.

2. Human Responsibility: Believers are entrusted with the ministry of reconciliation, implying that they are to actively engage in restoring relationships with others.

Reconciliation Among Believers

Paul's vision of reconciliation extends beyond the individual's relationship with God to include relationships within the Christian community. He consistently urged believers to live in harmony, forgive one another, and seek unity.

The Unity of the Body of Christ

In his letter to the Ephesians, Paul emphasizes the unity of believers in the body of Christ: "Make every effort to keep the unity of the Spirit through the bond of peace. There is one body and one Spirit, just as you were called to one hope when you were called; one Lord, one faith, one baptism; one God and Father of all, who is over all and through all and in all" (Ephesians 4:3-6). This call for unity underscores the importance of reconciliation in maintaining the integrity and witness of the Christian community.

The Role of Love in Reconciliation

Love is a central theme in Paul's theology of reconciliation. In 1 Corinthians 13, often referred to as the "love chapter," Paul describes love as the greatest of all virtues and essential for fostering healthy relationships. Love, as Paul describes it, is patient, kind, and forgiving. It does not keep a record of wrongs but seeks to restore and build up others.

Practical Expressions of Reconciliation in Paul's Ministry

The Case of Onesimus and Philemon

The letter to Philemon provides a concrete example of Paul's theology of reconciliation in action. Onesimus, a runaway slave, has become a Christian under Paul's mentorship. Paul writes to Philemon, Onesimus's master, urging him to receive Onesimus not as a slave but as a beloved brother in Christ.

Appeal for Forgiveness and Restoration

Paul's letter is a masterful blend of theological principles and pastoral care. He appeals to Philemon's faith and love, urging him to forgive Onesimus and to restore their relationship. Paul writes, "Perhaps the reason he was separated from you for a little while was that you might have him back forever—no longer as a slave, but better than a slave, as a dear brother" (Philemon 1:15-16). This appeal for the transformation of the master-slave relationship into one of brotherhood exemplifies the radical nature of Christian reconciliation.

Reconciliation in the Early Church

Paul's letters to the various Christian communities often addressed issues of division and conflict, providing guidance on how to achieve reconciliation.

Addressing Divisions in Corinth

The church in Corinth was plagued by divisions and conflicts. In his first letter to the Corinthians, Paul addresses these issues head-on, urging the believers to seek unity and reconciliation. He writes, "I appeal to you, brothers and sisters, in the name of our Lord Jesus Christ, that all of you agree with one another in what you say and that there be no divisions among you, but that you be perfectly united in mind and thought" (1 Corinthians 1:10). Paul's appeal underscores the importance of resolving conflicts and maintaining unity within the body of Christ.

Reconciliation between Jew and Gentile Believers

One of the significant challenges in the early church was reconciling Jewish and Gentile believers. In his letter to the Ephesians, Paul addresses this issue, emphasizing that Christ has broken down the dividing wall of hostility between the two groups. He writes, "For he himself is our peace, who has made the two groups one and has destroyed the barrier, the dividing wall of hostility" (Ephesians 2:14). This message of reconciliation highlights the inclusive nature of the gospel and the call for unity among all believers.

The Transformative Power of Reconciliation

Paul's theology of reconciliation is not merely theoretical but is intended to have a transformative impact on individuals and communities.

Personal Transformation

Reconciliation with God leads to a profound personal transformation. Paul describes this transformation in 2 Corinthians 5:17, stating, "Therefore, if anyone is in Christ, the new creation has come: The old has gone, the new is here!" This new creation involves a renewed relationship with God and a reoriented life characterized by love, forgiveness, and reconciliation.

Community Transformation

The transformative power of reconciliation extends to the Christian community. When believers practice reconciliation, it fosters a culture of peace, unity, and mutual support. This culture contrasts sharply with the divisive and often retributive nature of the broader society, offering a compelling witness to the power of the gospel.

Witness to the World

The reconciled community serves as a witness to the world of God's reconciling love. In John 13:35, Jesus tells His disciples, "By this everyone will know that you are my disciples, if you love one another." The practice of reconciliation within the Christian community demonstrates the reality of God's love and serves as a powerful testimony to the transformative impact of the gospel.

Paul's theology of reconciliation is a cornerstone of his writings and ministry. Rooted in the reconciling work of Christ, it calls for the restoration of broken relationships with God and among believers. Through his letters and pastoral care, Paul provides a comprehensive framework for understanding and practicing reconciliation, emphasizing its transformative power for individuals and communities.

By exploring Paul's theology of reconciliation, we gain valuable insights into the foundational principles of restorative justice within the Christian faith. These principles not only guide our understanding of justice and reconciliation but also inspire us to live out these values in our relationships and communities.

In the next chapter, we will delve into the specific strategies Paul used in his letter to Philemon to facilitate the reconciliation between Philemon and Onesimus. We will examine how these strategies reflect his theology of reconciliation and draw lessons for contemporary restorative justice practices.

CHAPTER 04

THE APPEAL OF PAUL

The Letter to Philemon: A Detailed Analysis

Paul's letter to Philemon stands out as a masterclass in gentle persuasion and restorative justice. It exemplifies how to address delicate interpersonal conflicts with a blend of commendation, heartfelt appeal, and personal commitment. By examining this letter in detail, we can uncover the specific strategies Paul used to facilitate the reconciliation between Philemon and Onesimus.

Structure and Overview of the Letter

Paul's letter to Philemon is composed of 25 verses and can be divided into several distinct sections: the greeting, commendation, the appeal for Onesimus, expressions of confidence, and final greetings. Each section plays a crucial role in Paul's overall strategy to persuade Philemon to forgive Onesimus and accept him as a brother in Christ.

Greeting (Verses 1-3)

Paul begins his letter with a warm and inclusive greeting:

Paul, a prisoner of Christ Jesus, and Timothy our brother,

To Philemon our dear friend and fellow worker—also to Apphia our sister and Archippus our fellow soldier—and to the church that meets in your home:

Grace and peace to you from God our Father and the Lord Jesus Christ.

This greeting sets a communal and respectful tone. By including Timothy, Apphia, Archippus, and the church, Paul emphasizes the collective nature of the Christian community and subtly underscores the communal implications of Philemon's decision regarding Onesimus.

Thanksgiving and Prayer (Verses 4-7)

Paul continues with a commendation of Philemon's faith and love:

I always thank my God as I remember you in my prayers because I hear about your love for all his holy people and your faith in the Lord Jesus. I pray that your partnership with us in the faith may be effective in deepening your understanding of every good thing we share for the sake of Christ. Your love has given me great joy and encouragement, because you, brother, have refreshed the hearts of the Lord's people.

By expressing gratitude and highlighting Philemon's virtues, Paul builds a foundation of mutual respect and goodwill. This section is not merely flattery; it serves to remind Philemon of his commitment to the Christian virtues of love and faith, setting the stage for the appeal that follows.

The Heartfelt Appeal (Verses 8-21)

The core of the letter is Paul's appeal for Onesimus:

Therefore, although in Christ I could be bold and order you to do what you ought to do, yet I prefer to appeal to you on the basis of love. It is as none other than Paul—an old man and now also a prisoner of Christ Jesus—that I appeal to you for my son Onesimus, who became my son while I was in chains. Formerly he was useless to you, but now he has become useful both to you and to me.

I am sending him—who is my very heart—back to you. I would have liked to keep him with me so that he could take your place in helping me while I am in chains for the gospel. But I did not want to do anything without your consent so that any favor you do would not seem forced but would be voluntary. Perhaps the reason he was separated from you for a little while was that you might have him back forever—no longer as a slave, but better than a slave, as a dear brother. He is very dear to me but even dearer to you, both as a fellow man and as a brother in the Lord.

So if you consider me a partner, welcome him as you would welcome me. If he has done you any wrong or owes you anything, charge it to me. I, Paul, am writing this with my own hand. I will pay it back—not to mention that you owe me your very self. I do wish, brother, that I may have some benefit from you in the Lord; refresh my heart in Christ. Confident of your obedience, I write to you, knowing that you will do even more than I ask.

Paul's appeal is multifaceted, blending personal affection, theological reasoning, and practical considerations.

1. Appealing on the Basis of Love: Paul chooses to appeal to Philemon's love rather than commanding him as an apostle. This approach respects Philemon's autonomy and encourages a voluntary, heartfelt response.

2. Transformation of Onesimus: Paul emphasizes the transformation Onesimus has undergone, describing him as a son and highlighting his newfound usefulness. This redefinition of Onesimus's identity is crucial for persuading Philemon to see him in a new light.

3. Personal Affection: By referring to Onesimus as "my very heart" and expressing a desire to keep him, Paul

conveys deep personal affection, which serves to humanize Onesimus and strengthen the emotional appeal.

4. Theological Implications: Paul hints at a divine purpose behind Onesimus's departure and return, suggesting that it was meant to transform their relationship from master-slave to brotherhood in Christ.

5. Offer of Restitution: Paul's offer to repay any debt Onesimus owes removes any financial barriers to reconciliation and demonstrates Paul's commitment to justice and restoration.

6. Subtle Pressure: While Paul refrains from commanding Philemon, he subtly reminds him of the debt he owes to Paul, creating a sense of moral obligation.

Expressions of Confidence (Verse 22)

Paul expresses confidence in Philemon's positive response:

And one thing more: Prepare a guest room for me, because I hope to be restored to you in answer to your prayers.

This expression of confidence serves multiple purposes. It indicates Paul's trust in Philemon's goodwill, reinforces their personal connection, and subtly implies that Paul will follow up on the situation, adding a gentle layer of accountability.

Final Greetings (Verses 23-25)

Paul concludes with personal greetings from his companions:

Epaphras, my fellow prisoner in Christ Jesus, sends you greetings. And so do Mark, Aristarchus, Demas and Luke, my fellow workers. The grace of the Lord Jesus Christ be with your spirit.

These final greetings reinforce the communal nature of the appeal and remind Philemon of the broader Christian fellowship that supports Paul's request.

The Strategic Use of Rhetoric

Paul's letter to Philemon is a strategic use of rhetoric aimed at achieving reconciliation through persuasion rather than coercion. His approach can be analyzed through several rhetorical techniques:

1. Ethos (Character and Credibility): Paul establishes his credibility by highlighting his relationship with both Philemon and Onesimus. His role as an apostle and a spiritual father lends weight to his appeal.

2. Pathos (Emotional Appeal): Paul's language is rich with emotional appeal. He speaks of Onesimus as his son and heart, evokes the image of Philemon's love and faith, and expresses personal longing for a positive outcome.

3. Logos (Logical Argument): Paul constructs a logical argument based on Onesimus's transformation and the theological implications of their new relationship in Christ. He uses reason to show why accepting Onesimus as a brother is the right course of action.

Implications for Restorative Justice

Paul's letter to Philemon offers valuable lessons for contemporary restorative justice practices:

1. Respect for Autonomy: Paul's approach respects Philemon's autonomy and encourages voluntary action, which is crucial for genuine reconciliation.

2. Emphasis on Transformation: Highlighting Onesimus's transformation underscores the potential for personal change and growth, a key aspect of restorative justice.

3. Personal Involvement: Paul's deep personal involvement and willingness to bear the cost of restitution reflect the importance of empathy and personal investment in the restorative process.

4. Community Support: The communal context of Paul's appeal demonstrates the role of the community in supporting reconciliation and ensuring accountability.

5. Balanced Appeal: Paul's blend of emotional, ethical, and logical appeals provides a balanced and holistic approach

to persuasion, essential for addressing complex interpersonal conflicts.

Paul's letter to Philemon is a profound example of how to address interpersonal conflicts with grace, empathy, and strategic persuasion. By analyzing this letter in detail, we can uncover timeless principles of restorative justice that continue to resonate in contemporary contexts. Paul's blend of commendation, heartfelt appeal, and personal commitment provides a powerful model for fostering reconciliation and restoring broken relationships.

In the next chapter, we will explore the key restorative justice techniques used by Paul in more depth, examining how these techniques can be applied in modern settings to promote healing and reconciliation.

PAUL'S TONE AND APPROACH

Paul's letter to Philemon is a masterful example of how to address sensitive interpersonal issues with warmth, respect, and strategic persuasion. His tone and approach in the letter are carefully crafted to foster reconciliation and mutual respect. By avoiding commands and instead appealing to Philemon's sense of Christian duty and love, Paul sets a powerful example of restorative justice in action.

Warm and Respectful Tone

Opening with Respect

From the very beginning of the letter, Paul establishes a tone of respect and warmth. He starts with a heartfelt greeting that includes not only Philemon but also Apphia, Archippus, and the church that meets in Philemon's home. This inclusive greeting sets a communal and respectful tone:

Paul, a prisoner of Christ Jesus, and Timothy our brother,

To Philemon our dear friend and fellow worker— also to Apphia our sister and Archippus our fellow soldier— and to the church that meets in your home:

Grace and peace to you from God our Father and the Lord Jesus Christ. (Philemon 1:1-3)

By addressing Philemon as a "dear friend and fellow worker," Paul acknowledges their shared mission and partnership in the gospel. This approach immediately establishes a sense of equality and mutual respect.

Commendation and Thanksgiving

Paul continues his letter with a section of thanksgiving and commendation:

I always thank my God as I remember you in my prayers, because I hear about your love for all his holy people and your faith in the Lord Jesus. I pray that your partnership with us in the faith may be effective in deepening your understanding of every good thing we share for the sake of Christ. Your love has given me great joy and encouragement, because you, brother, have refreshed the hearts of the Lord's people. (Philemon 1:4-7)

By expressing gratitude and highlighting Philemon's faith and love, Paul builds a foundation of mutual respect and goodwill. This commendation is not mere flattery but serves to remind Philemon of his Christian virtues and his positive impact on the community.

Avoiding Commands and Encouraging Voluntary Action

Appeal Instead of Command

One of the most striking aspects of Paul's approach is his decision to appeal to Philemon's sense of love and duty rather than issuing a command. Paul explicitly states this choice:

Therefore, although in Christ I could be bold and order you to do what you ought to do, yet I prefer to appeal to you on the basis of love. It is as none other than Paul—an old man and now also a prisoner of Christ Jesus—that I appeal to you for my son Onesimus, who became my son while I was in chains. (Philemon 1:8-10)

By choosing to appeal rather than command, Paul respects Philemon's autonomy and encourages a voluntary, heartfelt response. This approach aligns with the principles of restorative justice, which emphasize voluntary participation and mutual agreement.

Emphasizing Christian Duty and Love

Paul's appeal is grounded in the values of Christian duty and love. He reminds Philemon of the transformative power of the gospel and the new relationship that now exists between Philemon and Onesimus as brothers in Christ:

Perhaps the reason he was separated from you for a little while was that you might have him back forever—no longer as a slave, but better than a slave, as a dear brother. He is very dear to me but even dearer to you, both as a fellow man and as a brother in the Lord. (Philemon 1:15-16)

By framing the situation in terms of Christian duty and love, Paul encourages Philemon to act in accordance with his faith and values. This approach seeks to transform the master-slave relationship into one of brotherhood and mutual respect.

Addressing Philemon as a Friend and Fellow Worker

Building on Shared Values and Mission

Throughout the letter, Paul addresses Philemon as a friend and fellow worker in Christ. This language reinforces their shared values and mission, creating a sense of solidarity and partnership:

I do wish, brother, that I may have some benefit from you in the Lord; refresh my heart in Christ. Confident of your obedience, I write to you, knowing that you will do even more than I ask. (Philemon 1:20-21)

By referring to Philemon as a brother and expressing confidence in his response, Paul builds on their shared commitment to the gospel and the community. This approach fosters a sense of unity and encourages Philemon to respond positively.

Personal Commitment and Offer of Restitution

Paul's commitment to Onesimus's case is evident in his offer to make restitution for any wrongs Onesimus may have committed:

So if you consider me a partner, welcome him as you would welcome me. If he has done you any wrong or owes you anything, charge it to me. I, Paul, am writing this with my own hand. I will pay it back—not to mention that you owe me your very self. (Philemon 1:17-19)

By offering to repay any debt Onesimus owes, Paul removes any financial barriers to reconciliation and demonstrates his commitment to justice and restoration. This personal investment underscores the importance of empathy and solidarity in the restorative process.

The Strategic Use of Persuasion

Ethos (Character and Credibility)

Paul establishes his credibility by highlighting his relationship with both Philemon and Onesimus. His role as an apostle and a spiritual father lends weight to his appeal. By addressing Philemon with respect and acknowledging his virtues, Paul reinforces his own ethos as a compassionate and wise leader.

Pathos (Emotional Appeal)

Paul's language is rich with emotional appeal. He speaks of Onesimus as his son and heart, evokes the image of Philemon's love and faith, and expresses personal longing for a positive outcome. This emotional connection helps to humanize Onesimus and strengthen the appeal for forgiveness and reconciliation.

Logos (Logical Argument)

Paul constructs a logical argument based on Onesimus's transformation and the theological implications of their new relationship in Christ. He uses reason to show why accepting Onesimus as a brother is the right course of action. By framing the situation in terms of divine purpose and Christian duty, Paul makes a compelling case for reconciliation.

Paul's tone and approach in his letter to Philemon are masterful examples of how to address interpersonal conflicts with warmth, respect, and strategic persuasion. By avoiding commands and instead appealing to Philemon's sense of Christian duty and love, Paul sets a powerful example of restorative justice in action. His blend of commendation, heartfelt appeal, and personal commitment provides valuable lessons for fostering reconciliation and restoring broken relationships.

In the next chapter, we will delve into the key restorative justice techniques used by Paul in more depth, examining how these techniques can be applied in modern settings to promote healing and reconciliation.

THE REQUEST FOR OMESIMUS" FORGIVENESS AND RECONCILIATION

Paul's letter to Philemon centers on a radical and transformative request: that Philemon receive Onesimus not as a slave but as a beloved brother in Christ. This appeal not only challenges the prevailing social norms of the Roman Empire but also calls for a profound transformation in the relationship between Philemon and Onesimus. By examining Paul's request in detail, we can understand the depth of his approach to restorative justice and the implications it had for the early Christian community.

The Radical Nature of Paul's Request

Challenging Social Norms

In the Roman Empire, slavery was a deeply entrenched institution, and slaves were considered the property of their masters. The relationship between master and slave was one of dominance and subordination, with slaves having little to no rights. Paul's request that Philemon receive Onesimus as a brother rather than a slave was revolutionary. It directly challenged the established social order and called for a new way of relating to one another based on Christian principles.

Reframing Onesimus's Identity

Paul begins by reframing Onesimus's identity, emphasizing his transformation through Christ. He writes:

Formerly he was useless to you, but now he has become useful both to you and to me. (Philemon 1:11)

By highlighting Onesimus's newfound usefulness, Paul underscores the change that has occurred in Onesimus's life. This transformation is not merely practical but also spiritual, as Onesimus has become a valuable member of the Christian community.

Appeal to Christian Brotherhood

Paul's central request is encapsulated in his appeal to Philemon to receive Onesimus as a brother in Christ:

Perhaps the reason he was separated from you for a little while was that you might have him back forever—no longer as a slave, but better than a slave, as a dear brother. He is very dear to me but even dearer to you, both as a fellow man and as a brother in the Lord. (Philemon 1:15-16)

This appeal to Christian brotherhood is profound. It redefines the relationship between Philemon and Onesimus from one of master and slave to one of equals in the faith. This new relationship is based on mutual respect, love, and the shared identity of being members of the body of Christ.

The Theological Basis for Reconciliation

The New Creation in Christ

Paul's request is rooted in the theological concept of the new creation in Christ. He writes in 2 Corinthians 5:17:

Therefore, if anyone is in Christ, the new creation has come: The old has gone, the new is here!

This idea of a new creation emphasizes that believers are transformed through their faith in Christ. Old social distinctions and hierarchies are rendered obsolete, and new relationships are formed based on the equality and unity found in Christ.

The Ministry of Reconciliation

Paul's appeal also draws on the concept of the ministry of reconciliation, as outlined in 2 Corinthians 5:18-19:

All this is from God, who reconciled us to himself through Christ and gave us the ministry of reconciliation: that God was reconciling the world to himself in Christ, not counting people's sins against them. And he has committed to us the message of reconciliation.

By calling Philemon to reconcile with Onesimus, Paul is encouraging him to participate in this divine ministry of reconciliation. This involves not only forgiving Onesimus but also restoring him to a position of honor and equality within the Christian community.

Practical Steps for Reconciliation

Acknowledging Onesimus's Wrongdoing

Paul does not ignore the fact that Onesimus has wronged Philemon. He acknowledges the reality of the situation and offers a practical solution:

If he has done you any wrong or owes you anything, charge it to me. I, Paul, am writing this with my own hand. I will pay it back—not to mention that you owe me your very self. (Philemon 1:18-19)

By offering to make restitution on Onesimus's behalf, Paul addresses any potential financial or personal grievances that Philemon may have. This offer removes any barriers to forgiveness and emphasizes the importance of making amends in the process of reconciliation.

Encouraging Voluntary Action

Paul's approach is marked by a respect for Philemon's autonomy and a desire for voluntary action. He writes:

I did not want to do anything without your consent so any favor you did would not seem forced but would be voluntary. (Philemon 1:14)

This emphasis on voluntary action is crucial for genuine reconciliation. Paul seeks to create an environment where Philemon's decision to forgive and reconcile with Onesimus is motivated by love and a sense of Christian duty, rather than external pressure.

Building on Shared Faith and Values

Throughout his letter, Paul appeals to the shared faith and values that bind him, Philemon, and Onesimus together. He writes:

I do wish, brother, that I may have some benefit from you in the Lord; refresh my heart in Christ. Confident of your obedience, I write to you, knowing that you will do even more than I ask. (Philemon 1:20-21)

By framing his request within the context of their shared commitment to Christ, Paul reinforces the spiritual and moral basis for reconciliation. This shared faith provides a common ground that encourages Philemon to respond positively to Paul's appeal.

The Broader Implications for the Christian Community

Modeling Christian Reconciliation

Paul's request for Onesimus's forgiveness and reconciliation serves as a model for the broader Christian community. It demonstrates how believers are called to transcend societal norms and practice radical forgiveness and equality. This model of reconciliation has far-reaching implications for how conflicts and relationships are managed within the church.

Promoting Unity and Inclusivity

By advocating for Onesimus's acceptance as a brother, Paul promotes the principles of unity and inclusivity within the Christian community. This approach challenges the existing social hierarchies and emphasizes the inclusive nature of the gospel. It encourages the early Christians to see each other as equals, regardless of their social or economic status.

Strengthening the Witness of the Church

The reconciliation between Philemon and Onesimus would have strengthened the witness of the early church. It would have demonstrated to the wider society the transformative power of the gospel in breaking down barriers and fostering genuine community. This powerful example of reconciliation would have served as a testimony to the love and unity that characterized the Christian faith.

Paul's central request in his letter to Philemon is a radical appeal for forgiveness and reconciliation that challenges social norms and calls for a profound transformation in the relationship between Philemon and Onesimus. By asking Philemon to receive Onesimus as a beloved brother, Paul redefines their relationship and sets a powerful example of restorative justice in action.

This appeal is grounded in the theological principles of the new creation in Christ and the ministry of reconciliation. It emphasizes the importance of voluntary action, making amends, and building on shared faith and values. The broader implications of this request highlight the need for unity, inclusivity, and the strengthening of the church's witness.

In the next chapter, we will explore the key restorative justice techniques used by Paul in more depth, examining how these techniques can be applied in modern settings to promote healing and reconciliation. By understanding these techniques, we can draw valuable lessons for contemporary restorative justice practices and their potential to transform relationships and communities.

CHAPTER 05

KEY RESTORATIVE JUSTICE TECHNIQUES USED BY PAUL

Paul's letter to Philemon not only advocates for reconciliation but also exemplifies several key restorative justice techniques. Among these techniques, empathy and compassion stand out as fundamental components of Paul's approach. By showing deep empathy for Onesimus and acknowledging his past wrongs while recognizing his potential and new identity in Christ, Paul sets a powerful example of how restorative justice can transform relationships and promote healing.

Empathy and Compassion

Paul's Empathy for Onesimus

Paul's empathy for Onesimus is evident throughout his letter to Philemon. Rather than simply advocating for

Onesimus as a theoretical case, Paul speaks of him with deep personal affection and understanding.

Acknowledging Onesimus's Past Wrongs

Paul does not ignore the fact that Onesimus has wronged Philemon. He acknowledges the reality of the situation, which is crucial for maintaining honesty and integrity in the process of reconciliation:

If he has done you any wrong or owes you anything, charge it to me. (Philemon 1:18)

By addressing the wrongs Onesimus has committed, Paul demonstrates his understanding of the impact of these actions on Philemon. This acknowledgment is a critical step in validating Philemon's feelings and experiences, which is essential for genuine reconciliation.

Recognizing Onesimus's Potential and New Identity

While Paul acknowledges Onesimus's past wrongs, he places greater emphasis on Onesimus's potential and his new identity in Christ. Paul writes:

Formerly he was useless to you, but now he has become useful both to you and to me. (Philemon 1:11)

This statement highlights the transformation that has taken place in Onesimus's life. Paul sees Onesimus not just as a runaway slave but as a valuable member of the Christian community. By recognizing Onesimus's potential and new identity, Paul encourages Philemon to look beyond past transgressions and see the possibility of a renewed relationship.

Encouraging Philemon's Compassion

Appealing to Love and Brotherhood

Paul's appeal to Philemon is grounded in the principles of love and brotherhood. He urges Philemon to view Onesimus not as a slave but as a brother in Christ:

Perhaps the reason he was separated from you for a little while was that you might have him back forever—no longer as a slave, but better than a slave, as a dear brother. He is very dear to me but even dearer to you, both as a fellow man and as a brother in the Lord. (Philemon 1:15-16)

By framing Onesimus's return in terms of brotherhood, Paul calls on Philemon to exercise compassion and embrace Onesimus as an equal in the faith. This appeal to love and brotherhood is designed to evoke empathy and a willingness to forgive.

Personal Investment in Onesimus's Future

Paul's willingness to invest personally in Onesimus's future further underscores his compassionate approach. He offers to take responsibility for any debts Onesimus owes:

If he has done you any wrong or owes you anything, charge it to me. I, Paul, am writing this with my own hand. I will pay it back—not to mention that you owe me your very self. (Philemon 1:18-19)

This offer not only removes potential barriers to reconciliation but also demonstrates Paul's deep commitment to Onesimus's well-being. By investing personally in Onesimus's future, Paul sets an example of the kind of sacrificial love and support that is central to restorative justice.

Mediation and Advocacy

Paul as a Mediator

Paul's role as a mediator is crucial in facilitating the reconciliation between Philemon and Onesimus. As a respected apostle and a spiritual father to both men, Paul leverages his position to bring about a resolution that honors their shared faith and values.

Building Trust and Communication

Effective mediation requires building trust and facilitating open communication. Paul's letter serves as a bridge between Philemon and Onesimus, creating a space for dialogue and understanding. By expressing his confidence in Philemon's character and appealing to his sense of Christian duty, Paul fosters an environment conducive to reconciliation:

Confident of your obedience, I write to you, knowing that you will do even more than I ask. (Philemon 1:21)

This expression of confidence helps to build trust and encourages Philemon to respond positively.

The Role of Advocacy in Restorative Justice

As an advocate for Onesimus, Paul goes beyond mediation to actively support Onesimus's case. He speaks on behalf of Onesimus, highlighting his transformation and potential, and takes on any financial liabilities to remove obstacles to reconciliation. This advocacy is a key component of restorative justice, emphasizing the need to support and empower those who seek to make amends.

Reconciliation and Forgiveness

The Call for Forgiveness

Paul's central request is for Philemon to forgive Onesimus and to receive him as a brother in Christ. This call for forgiveness is rooted in the transformative power of the gospel and the new relationships it creates:

So, if you consider me a partner, welcome him as you would welcome me. (Philemon 1:17)

By asking Philemon to welcome Onesimus as he would welcome Paul himself, Paul emphasizes the importance of forgiveness and the restoration of relationships within the Christian community.

Steps Towards Reconciliation

Reconciliation is not a one-time event but a process that involves several steps. Paul outlines these steps in his letter, providing a framework for Philemon to follow:

1. Acknowledging the Wrong: Paul acknowledges the wrongs committed by Onesimus and offers restitution.

2. Transforming Relationships: Paul calls for a transformation in the relationship between Philemon and Onesimus, from master-slave to brothers in Christ.

3. Building on Shared Values: Paul appeals to the shared faith and values of the Christian community, encouraging Philemon to act out of love and duty.

4. Personal Commitment: Paul's personal investment in Onesimus's future demonstrates the importance of support and commitment in the reconciliation process.

Restitution and Restoration

Paul's Offer to Repay

Restitution is a key component of restorative justice, aimed at repairing the harm caused by wrongdoing. Paul's offer to repay any debts Onesimus owes is a concrete example of this principle in action:

If he has done you any wrong or owes you anything, charge it to me. (Philemon 1:18)

This offer not only addresses the financial aspect of the wrong but also demonstrates Paul's commitment to justice and restoration. It removes any remaining barriers to reconciliation and emphasizes the importance of making amends.

The Principle of Restitution in Restorative Justice

Restitution goes beyond mere compensation; it is about restoring relationships and rebuilding trust. By offering restitution, Paul acknowledges the harm caused and takes steps to repair it. This principle is central to restorative justice, which seeks to heal and restore rather than simply punish.

Paul's letter to Philemon is a powerful example of restorative justice in action. Through his empathy and compassion, mediation and advocacy, call for forgiveness, and offer of restitution, Paul demonstrates how to address wrongdoing and promote healing and reconciliation. His approach highlights the importance of seeing the potential for transformation in others and the power of the gospel to create new relationships based on love, equality, and mutual respect.

In the next chapter, we will explore the broader impact of Paul's intervention on Onesimus, Philemon, and the early Christian community. By understanding the outcomes of this reconciliation, we can gain further insights into the transformative power of restorative justice and its relevance for contemporary contexts.

MEDIATION AND ADVOCACY

Paul's letter to Philemon not only embodies the principles of restorative justice but also showcases the vital roles of mediation and advocacy. As a mediator, Paul facilitates communication and understanding between Philemon and Onesimus. Additionally, his advocacy for Onesimus highlights the importance of supporting and empowering individuals seeking reconciliation. This chapter explores Paul's dual roles and their significance in the context of restorative justice.

Paul as a Mediator

Facilitating Communication and Understanding

Mediation is a critical component of restorative justice, aimed at resolving conflicts and fostering mutual understanding. In the case of Philemon and Onesimus, Paul steps into the role of mediator, bridging the gap between the two parties and facilitating a dialogue that promotes reconciliation.

Establishing a Respectful Tone

Paul's mediation begins with the establishment of a respectful and empathetic tone. He addresses Philemon with honor and gratitude, acknowledging his contributions to the Christian community:

I always thank my God as I remember you in my prayers because I hear about your love for all his holy people and your faith in the Lord Jesus. (Philemon 1:4-5)

This respectful approach sets the stage for a constructive dialogue, emphasizing mutual respect and the shared values of the Christian faith.

Highlighting Shared Interests

A key aspect of effective mediation is identifying and emphasizing shared interests. Paul highlights the common ground between Philemon and Onesimus by focusing on their shared faith and commitment to Christ. He writes:

Perhaps the reason he was separated from you for a little while was that you might have him back forever—no longer as a slave, but better than a slave, as a dear brother. He is very dear to me but even dearer to you, both as a fellow man and as a brother in the Lord. (Philemon 1:15-16)

By framing Onesimus's return in terms of brotherhood and mutual benefit, Paul encourages Philemon to view the situation from a perspective of shared interests and values.

Encouraging Open Communication

Effective mediation also involves encouraging open communication and providing a platform for both parties to express their perspectives. While Paul speaks on behalf of Onesimus, he also creates space for Philemon to respond and make his own decisions. This approach respects Philemon's autonomy and fosters an environment where genuine dialogue can occur.

Building Trust and Accountability

Trust and accountability are essential elements of mediation. Paul builds trust by demonstrating his own commitment to the reconciliation process and by holding himself accountable for any restitution required.

Personal Commitment and Accountability

Paul's offer to bear any financial restitution owed by Onesimus is a significant demonstration of his personal commitment to the reconciliation process:

If he has done you any wrong or owes you anything, charge it to me. I, Paul, am writing this with my own hand. I will pay it back—not to mention that you owe me your very self. (Philemon 1:18-19)

By offering to repay any debts, Paul removes potential barriers to reconciliation and underscores his dedication to justice and restoration. This personal investment helps to build trust and reassures Philemon of Paul's sincerity.

Confidence in Positive Outcomes

Paul expresses confidence in Philemon's positive response, which serves to reinforce trust and encourage a favorable outcome:

Confident of your obedience, I write to you, knowing that you will do even more than I ask. (Philemon 1:21)

This expression of confidence not only shows Paul's trust in Philemon's character but also motivates Philemon to live up to the expectations of his faith and values.

The Role of Advocacy in Restorative Justice

Advocating for Onesimus

Advocacy is a crucial aspect of restorative justice, aimed at supporting and empowering individuals who seek to make amends and rebuild relationships. Paul's advocacy for Onesimus is evident throughout his letter, as he speaks on Onesimus's behalf and emphasizes his transformation.

Emphasizing Transformation and Potential

Paul advocates for Onesimus by highlighting his transformation and a new identity in Christ. He writes:

Formerly he was useless to you, but now he has become useful both to you and to me. (Philemon 1:11)

By focusing on Onesimus's newfound usefulness and potential, Paul encourages Philemon to see beyond past transgressions and recognize the positive changes in

Onesimus's character. This emphasis on transformation is a key element of restorative justice, which seeks to rehabilitate and restore individuals rather than simply punish them.

Personal Testimony and Support

Paul's testimony about Onesimus adds weight to his advocacy. He speaks of Onesimus with deep affection and respect, referring to him as "my son" and "my very heart":

I appeal to you for my son Onesimus, who became my son while I was in chains. (Philemon 1:10)

I am sending him—who is my very heart—back to you. (Philemon 1:12)

These personal endorsements serve to humanize Onesimus and present him as a valued and beloved member of the Christian community. Paul's support helps to build a positive narrative around Onesimus and advocates for his acceptance and reintegration.

Supporting the Process of Reconciliation

Advocacy in restorative justice also involves supporting the overall process of reconciliation, ensuring that both parties have the resources and support they need to move forward.

Offering Restitution and Repairing Harm

Paul's offer to make restitution for any wrongs committed by Onesimus is a critical aspect of his advocacy:

If he has done you any wrong or owes you anything, charge it to me. (Philemon 1:18)

This offer addresses the practical aspects of reconciliation by removing financial barriers and demonstrating a commitment to repairing harm. Restitution is a vital component of restorative justice, as it helps to restore trust and balance in the relationship.

Encouraging Forgiveness and Restoration

Paul's advocacy also involves encouraging Philemon to forgive Onesimus and to restore their relationship based on Christian principles of love and brotherhood:

So if you consider me a partner, welcome him as you would welcome me. (Philemon 1:17)

By framing the request for reconciliation in terms of their shared faith and partnership, Paul reinforces the importance of forgiveness and the transformative power of the gospel. His advocacy promotes a holistic approach to justice that prioritizes healing and restoration.

Paul's roles as a mediator and advocate in his letter to Philemon provide a powerful example of restorative justice in action. As a mediator, Paul facilitates communication and understanding between Philemon and Onesimus, building trust and fostering a respectful dialogue. As an advocate, he supports Onesimus's case, highlighting his transformation and offering to bear any financial restitution required.

These roles demonstrate the importance of empathy, support, and personal investment in the process of reconciliation. By advocating for restorative justice principles, Paul sets a precedent for how conflicts can be resolved through understanding, forgiveness, and the restoration of relationships.

In the next chapter, we will explore the broader impact of Paul's intervention on Onesimus, Philemon, and the early Christian community. By understanding the outcomes of this reconciliation, we can gain further insights into the transformative power of restorative justice and its relevance for contemporary contexts.

RECONCILIATION AND FORGIVENESS

Reconciliation and forgiveness are at the heart of Paul's letter to Philemon. Through his appeal, Paul calls for Philemon to forgive Onesimus, reflecting the forgiveness that believers receive from Christ. Additionally, Paul outlines concrete steps towards reconciliation, emphasizing the importance of receiving Onesimus warmly and treating him as a brother. This chapter delves into Paul's call for forgiveness and the practical steps he advocates for achieving true reconciliation.

The Call for Forgiveness

Reflecting Christ's Forgiveness

Paul's call for Philemon to forgive Onesimus is deeply rooted in the Christian understanding of forgiveness as a reflection of the grace believers receive from Christ. Paul writes:

Therefore, although in Christ I could be bold and order you to do what you ought to do, yet I prefer to appeal to you based on love. (Philemon 1:8-9)

Paul emphasizes that his appeal is grounded in love, mirroring the love and forgiveness that Christ extends to all believers. This approach highlights the theological foundation of forgiveness in the Christian faith, where forgiveness is not merely a moral obligation but a response to the grace received from God.

Emphasizing Equality and Brotherhood

Paul urges Philemon to transcend the traditional master-slave relationship and embrace Onesimus as a brother in Christ. He writes:

Perhaps the reason he was separated from you for a little while was that you might have him back forever—no longer as a slave, but better than a slave, as a dear brother. He is very dear to me but even dearer to you, both as a fellow man and as a brother in the Lord. (Philemon 1:15-16)

By framing Onesimus's return in terms of brotherhood, Paul calls for a fundamental shift in the way Philemon views Onesimus. This appeal to equality and brotherhood reflects the transformative power of the gospel, which breaks down social barriers and creates new relationships based on mutual respect and love.

Forgiveness as a Path to Reconciliation

Paul's call for forgiveness is not an end in itself but a pathway to reconciliation. Forgiveness serves as the foundation for restoring broken relationships and healing past wounds. By forgiving Onesimus, Philemon can begin the process of rebuilding trust and fostering a renewed relationship based on their shared faith.

Steps Towards Reconciliation

Receiving Onesimus Warmly

The first practical step towards reconciliation that Paul advocates is for Philemon to receive Onesimus warmly. He writes:

So if you consider me a partner, welcome him as you would welcome me. (Philemon 1:17)

This step is crucial because it sets the tone for the entire reconciliation process. By welcoming Onesimus warmly, Philemon can demonstrate his willingness to move past the transgressions and embrace Onesimus as a valued member of the community. This act of hospitality reflects the inclusive nature of the Christian faith and the importance of creating a supportive and welcoming environment for all believers.

Treating Onesimus as a Brother

Paul's request that Philemon treat Onesimus as a brother goes beyond mere forgiveness. It calls for a profound transformation in their relationship. Paul emphasizes this point by stating:

No longer as a slave, but better than a slave, as a dear brother. (Philemon 1:16)

This redefinition of their relationship challenges the existing social norms and calls for a new way of relating to one another. Treating Onesimus as a brother involves recognizing his inherent worth and dignity as a fellow believer, which is essential for true reconciliation.

Acknowledging and Addressing the Past

Effective reconciliation requires acknowledging and addressing past wrongs. Paul does not ignore the fact that Onesimus has wronged Philemon. Instead, he acknowledges it and offers to make restitution:

If he has done you any wrong or owes you anything, charge it to me. I, Paul, am writing this with my own hand. I will pay it back. (Philemon 1:18-19)

By addressing the past, Paul ensures that any lingering issues are resolved, paving the way for a fresh start. This step is critical because it validates Philemon's feelings and experiences while demonstrating a commitment to justice and restoration.

Encouraging Voluntary Action

Paul emphasizes the importance of voluntary action in the reconciliation process. He writes:

I did not want to do anything without your consent so any favor you did would not seem forced but would be voluntary. (Philemon 1:14)

By encouraging Philemon to act voluntarily, Paul respects his autonomy and ensures that the reconciliation process is genuine and heartfelt. This approach aligns with the principles of restorative justice, which prioritize voluntary participation and mutual agreement.

Building on Shared Faith and Values

Throughout his letter, Paul appeals to the shared faith and values that bind him, Philemon, and Onesimus together. He writes:

I do wish, brother, that I may have some benefit from you in the Lord; refresh my heart in Christ. Confident of your obedience, I write to you, knowing that you will do even more than I ask. (Philemon 1:20-21)

By framing his request within the context of their shared commitment to Christ, Paul reinforces the spiritual and moral basis for reconciliation. This shared faith provides a common ground that encourages Philemon to respond positively and act in accordance with Christian principles of love, forgiveness, and brotherhood.

The Broader Implications for the Christian Community

Modeling Christian Reconciliation

Paul's request for Onesimus's forgiveness and reconciliation serves as a model for the broader Christian community. It demonstrates how believers are called to transcend societal norms and practice radical forgiveness and equality. This model of reconciliation has far-reaching implications for how conflicts and relationships are managed within the church.

Promoting Unity and Inclusivity

By advocating for Onesimus's acceptance as a brother, Paul promotes the principles of unity and inclusivity within the Christian community. This approach challenges existing social hierarchies and emphasizes the inclusive nature of the gospel. It encourages early Christians to see each other as equals, regardless of their social or economic status.

Strengthening the Witness of the Church

The reconciliation between Philemon and Onesimus would have strengthened the witness of the early church. It would have demonstrated to the wider society the transformative power of the gospel in breaking down barriers and fostering genuine community. This powerful example of reconciliation would have served as a testimony to the love and unity that characterized the Christian faith.

Paul's letter to Philemon is a profound example of how to address interpersonal conflicts with grace, empathy, and strategic persuasion. By calling for Philemon to forgive Onesimus and outlining concrete steps towards reconciliation, Paul sets a powerful example of restorative justice in action. His approach highlights the importance of seeing the potential for transformation in others and the power of the gospel to create new relationships based on love, equality, and mutual respect.

In the next chapter, we will explore the broader impact of Paul's intervention on Onesimus, Philemon, and the early Christian community. By understanding the outcomes of this reconciliation, we can gain further insights into the transformative power of restorative justice and its relevance for contemporary contexts.

RESTITUTION AND RESTORATION

Restitution and restoration are central themes in Paul's letter to Philemon. By offering to repay any debt Onesimus owes, Paul embodies the principle of restitution and demonstrates the importance of making amends in the process of reconciliation. This chapter explores Paul's offer of restitution and the broader principle of restitution in restorative justice, emphasizing its role in repairing harm and restoring relationships.

Paul's Offer to Repay

Embodying the Principle of Restitution

Paul's offer to repay any debt Onesimus owes to Philemon is a tangible expression of his commitment to justice and reconciliation. He writes:

If he has done you any wrong or owes you anything, charge it to me. I, Paul, am writing this with my own hand. I will pay it back—not to mention that you owe me your very self. (Philemon 1:18-19)

By taking on Onesimus's debt, Paul removes a significant barrier to reconciliation. This act of restitution serves several important functions:

Acknowledging the Harm

First, Paul's offer acknowledges that harm has been done and that it needs to be addressed. This acknowledgment is crucial for validating Philemon's experience and ensuring that the reconciliation process is built on a foundation of truth and accountability.

Demonstrating Commitment to Justice

Second, Paul's willingness to make restitution demonstrates his commitment to justice. It shows that he is not merely advocating for Onesimus out of personal affection but is also committed to addressing the wrongs that have been committed and ensuring that justice is served.

Facilitating Reconciliation

Third, by offering to repay the debt, Paul facilitates the reconciliation process. His offer removes any financial obstacles that might hinder Philemon's ability to forgive and reconcile with Onesimus. This practical step paves the way for a renewed relationship based on mutual respect and trust.

The Cost of Reconciliation

Paul's offer to repay any debt highlights the cost of reconciliation. True reconciliation often requires personal sacrifice and a willingness to bear the cost of making things right. In this case, Paul's offer of restitution is a powerful demonstration of his dedication to the principles of restorative justice and his commitment to the well-being of both Onesimus and Philemon.

The Principle of Restitution in Restorative Justice

A Key Component of Restorative Justice

Restitution is a key component of restorative justice, which aims to repair harm and restore relationships. Unlike retributive justice, which focuses on punishment, restorative justice seeks to address the needs of victims, offenders, and the community by encouraging accountability and making amends.

Repairing Harm

Restitution involves taking responsibility for the harm caused and taking concrete steps to repair that harm. This can take many forms, including financial compensation, community service, or personal apologies. The goal is to acknowledge the impact of the wrongdoing and to take actions that help to heal the wounds and restore trust.

Personal Responsibility and Accountability

Restitution requires the offender to take personal responsibility for their actions and to actively participate in the process of making things right. This emphasis on accountability is essential for fostering genuine repentance and promoting personal growth and transformation.

Restoring Relationships

Restitution is not just about addressing the immediate harm; it is also about restoring relationships. By making amends, the offender demonstrates their commitment to rebuilding trust and repairing the relational damage caused by their actions.

The Role of the Community

In restorative justice, the community plays a vital role in the restitution process. The community provides support and accountability for both the victim and the offender, ensuring that the process is fair and that the needs of all parties are addressed. This communal involvement helps to reinforce social bonds and promote a sense of collective responsibility for maintaining justice and harmony.

The Transformative Power of Restitution

Restitution has the potential to transform individuals and relationships. For the offender, taking responsibility and making amends can be a powerful catalyst for personal growth and rehabilitation. For the victim, receiving restitution can provide a sense of closure and validation, helping to heal emotional wounds and restore a sense of justice.

Restitution in the Biblical Context

The principle of restitution is deeply rooted in the biblical context. In the Old Testament, the Law of Moses includes numerous provisions for restitution, emphasizing the importance of making amends for wrongs committed. For example, in Exodus 22:1, it is stated:

Whoever steals an ox or a sheep and slaughters it or sells it must pay back five head of cattle for the ox and four sheep for the sheep.

These laws reflect the biblical emphasis on justice, accountability, and the restoration of relationships. Paul's offer of restitution in his letter to Philemon can be seen as an extension of this biblical principle, applied within the context of the early Christian community.

The Broader Implications for the Christian Community

Modeling Restorative Justice

Paul's approach to restitution in his letter to Philemon serves as a model for the broader Christian community. It demonstrates how believers can embody the principles of restorative justice in their relationships, addressing harm and seeking to restore trust and harmony.

Promoting a Culture of Accountability and Compassion

By emphasizing restitution and restoration, the Christian community can promote a culture of accountability and compassion. This culture encourages individuals to take responsibility for their actions, seek forgiveness, and make amends, while also fostering an environment of support and empathy.

Strengthening the Witness of the Church

The practice of restitution and restoration within the Christian community strengthens the church's witness to the transformative power of the gospel. It provides a tangible example of how the principles of justice, forgiveness, and reconciliation can be lived out in everyday relationships, demonstrating the distinctive nature of the Christian faith.

Restitution and restoration are central themes in Paul's letter to Philemon. Through his offer to repay any debt Onesimus owes, Paul embodies the principle of restitution and demonstrates the importance of making amends in the process of reconciliation. This act of restitution serves to acknowledge the harm done, demonstrate a commitment to justice, and facilitate the process of reconciliation.

The broader principle of restitution in restorative justice emphasizes the need to repair harm and restore relationships, promoting accountability, healing, and transformation. By modeling these principles, the Christian community can foster a culture of accountability and compassion, strengthening its witness to the transformative power of the gospel.

In the next chapter, we will explore the broader impact of Paul's intervention on Onesimus, Philemon, and the early Christian community. By understanding the outcomes of this reconciliation, we can gain further insights into the transformative power of restorative justice and its relevance for contemporary contexts.

CHAPTER 06

THE OUTCOME OF PAUL'S INTERVENTION

Paul's intervention in the relationship between Philemon and Onesimus stands as a powerful example of restorative justice at work. The outcome of this intervention had profound implications for Onesimus, Philemon, and the broader Christian community. This chapter focuses on the impact of Paul's intervention on Onesimus, exploring how it transformed his status and relationship with Philemon and provided a path to a new beginning.

The Impact on Onesimus

Transformation of Status

One of the most significant outcomes of Paul's intervention is the transformation of Onesimus's status. Previously, Onesimus was a runaway slave, a position that carried with it a social stigma and the threat of severe punishment. By advocating for Onesimus and appealing to

Philemon to receive him as a brother, Paul fundamentally changed Onesimus's standing within the Christian community.

From Slave to Brother

Paul explicitly calls for Philemon to regard Onesimus no longer as a slave but as a beloved brother in Christ:

Perhaps the reason he was separated from you for a little while was that you might have him back forever—no longer as a slave, but better than a slave, as a dear brother. (Philemon 1:15-16)

This redefinition of Onesimus's status represents a radical shift from the prevailing social norms of the Roman Empire, where slaves were considered property. By elevating Onesimus to the status of a brother, Paul underscores the Christian principle of equality and the transformative power of the gospel.

Recognition of Dignity and Worth

In advocating for Onesimus's new status, Paul also affirms his inherent dignity and worth. This recognition is crucial for Onesimus's self-identity and for how he is perceived by others in the community. It shifts the narrative from one of subjugation to one of mutual respect and love.

Restoration of Relationship

Paul's intervention also aimed at restoring the broken relationship between Onesimus and Philemon. This restoration involved several key components:

Forgiveness and Reconciliation

Central to the restoration of their relationship was the call for forgiveness. Paul urges Philemon to forgive Onesimus for any wrongs he has committed and to embrace him as a brother. This act of forgiveness is essential for healing past wounds and moving forward in a renewed relationship.

So, if you consider me a partner, welcome him as you would welcome me. (Philemon 1:17)

Rebuilding Trust

Restoring the relationship between Onesimus and Philemon also required rebuilding trust. Paul's offer to repay any debt Onesimus owed was a critical step in this process. By addressing any potential financial grievances, Paul removed barriers to reconciliation and laid the groundwork for trust to be reestablished.

If he has done you any wrong or owes you anything, charge it to me. I, Paul, am writing this with my hand. I will pay it back. (Philemon 1:18-19)

New Beginnings

Paul's appeal provided Onesimus with an opportunity for a new beginning. By reintroducing Onesimus to Philemon in the context of their shared faith and values, Paul created a pathway for a fresh start. This new beginning was not just about resuming their previous relationship but about forging a new relationship based on mutual respect, love, and brotherhood.

Empowerment and Personal Growth

Paul's intervention empowered Onesimus in several ways:

Affirmation of Identity

By affirming Onesimus's new identity in Christ, Paul empowered him to see himself in a new light. This affirmation was crucial for Onesimus's self-esteem and his sense of belonging within the Christian community. It provided a foundation for personal growth and transformation.

Encouragement and Support

Paul's affection and support for Onesimus were also empowering. By referring to Onesimus as "my son" and "my very heart," Paul offered encouragement and a sense of worth that were likely transformative for Onesimus.

I appeal to you for my son Onesimus, who became my son while I was in chains. (Philemon 1:10)

I am sending him—who is my very heart—back to you. (Philemon 1:12)

Implications for Onesimus's Future

The impact of Paul's intervention extended beyond the immediate reconciliation with Philemon. It had significant implications for Onesimus's future:

Reintegration into the Community

By facilitating reconciliation and transforming Onesimus's status, Paul helped pave the way for his reintegration into the Christian community. This reintegration was essential for Onesimus's social and spiritual well-being, providing him with a supportive network and a sense of belonging.

Potential for Leadership

The transformation of Onesimus's status and his positive relationship with Paul may have opened up opportunities for leadership within the Christian community. Onesimus's story of transformation and reconciliation could serve as a powerful testimony and example for others, potentially positioning him for roles of influence and service within the church.

Long-Term Impact

The long-term impact of Paul's intervention on Onesimus's life is not fully documented in the New Testament. However, early Christian tradition suggests that Onesimus went on to become a bishop in Ephesus, highlighting the lasting influence of Paul's advocacy and the transformative power of reconciliation.

Lessons for Contemporary Restorative Justice

Paul's intervention in the case of Onesimus and Philemon offers valuable lessons for contemporary restorative justice practices:

The Power of Advocacy

Paul's role as an advocate for Onesimus underscores the importance of advocacy in restorative justice. Advocates play a crucial role in supporting individuals who seek to make amends and facilitating the reconciliation process.

The Importance of Restitution

Paul's offer to repay any debt owed by Onesimus highlights the significance of restitution in repairing harm and restoring relationships. Restitution is a key component of restorative justice, emphasizing accountability and the need to make amends.

The Transformative Potential of Reconciliation

The transformation of Onesimus's status and relationship with Philemon illustrates the transformative potential of reconciliation. Restorative justice aims to heal and restore, creating opportunities for new beginnings and personal growth.

Paul's intervention in the relationship between Philemon and Onesimus had a profound impact on Onesimus's status, relationship with Philemon, and future within the Christian community. By advocating for Onesimus and facilitating reconciliation, Paul transformed a runaway slave into a beloved brother, providing a path to a new beginning and empowering Onesimus for personal growth and potential leadership.

The principles of advocacy, restitution, and reconciliation demonstrated in this case offer valuable insights for contemporary restorative justice practices. They highlight the transformative power of addressing harm, making amends, and fostering relationships based on mutual respect, love, and equality.

In the next chapter, we will explore the impact of Paul's intervention on Philemon, examining how it challenged social norms and influenced his faith and actions. By understanding Philemon's perspective, we can gain a more comprehensive view of the broader implications of restorative justice within the early Christian community and beyond.

THE IMPACT OF PHILEMON

Paul's appeal to Philemon not only aimed to transform the status and relationship of Onesimus but also had a significant impact on Philemon himself. The request challenged Philemon to practice Christian forgiveness and reconciliation, thereby deepening his faith and strengthening his relationships within the Christian community. This chapter explores how Paul's intervention influenced Philemon, prompting him to embody the principles of restorative justice and Christian love.

The Challenge of Forgiveness and Reconciliation

A Call to Practice Christian Virtues

Paul's letter to Philemon is a call to practice the core Christian virtues of forgiveness, love, and reconciliation. Philemon, as a prominent member of the Christian community in Colossae, was well-regarded for his faith and generosity. Paul acknowledges this at the beginning of his letter:

I always thank my God as I remember you in my prayers because I hear about your love for all his holy people and your faith in the Lord Jesus. (Philemon 1:4-5)

However, Paul's appeal presented a specific and personal challenge to Philemon: to forgive Onesimus, a runaway slave who had wronged him, and to receive him not as a slave but as a brother in Christ.

Overcoming Social Norms

Philemon's willingness to forgive Onesimus required him to transcend the social norms of the Roman Empire, where slaves were considered property and their masters had absolute authority over them. By asking Philemon to accept Onesimus as a brother, Paul was challenging him to adopt a radically different perspective, one that was grounded in the transformative power of the gospel.

Perhaps the reason he was separated from you for a little while was that you might have him back forever—no longer as a slave, but better than a slave, as a dear brother. (Philemon 1:15-16)

The Difficulty of Genuine Forgiveness

Forgiving Onesimus was not a simple or easy task. It required Philemon to let go of any anger, resentment, or desire for retribution. Genuine forgiveness involves a deep emotional and spiritual process, where the wronged party releases their hold on the past and opens their heart to reconciliation.

Deepening of Faith

A Test of Christian Maturity

Paul's request was a test of Philemon's Christian maturity. It required Philemon to live out the teachings of Jesus in a very concrete and personal way. Jesus emphasized the importance of forgiveness and reconciliation in His ministry, teaching His followers to forgive others as they have been forgiven by God.

For if you forgive other people when they sin against you, your heavenly Father will also forgive you. But if you do not forgive others their sins, your Father will not forgive your sins. (Matthew 6:14-15)

By responding to Paul's appeal with forgiveness and reconciliation, Philemon would be demonstrating his growth in faith and his commitment to living out the gospel.

Strengthening of Personal Faith

Forgiving Onesimus and embracing him as a brother in Christ would have deepened Philemon's faith. This act of forgiveness would have required Philemon to rely on God's grace and strength, recognizing his own need for forgiveness and extending that grace to Onesimus. This reliance on God in the process of reconciliation would have strengthened Philemon's relationship with God and his understanding of God's love and mercy.

Strengthening Relationships

Restored Relationship with Onesimus

The most immediate impact of Philemon's forgiveness would have been the restoration of his relationship with Onesimus. This restored relationship, based on mutual respect and brotherhood, would have been a powerful testament to the transformative power of the gospel.

Enhanced Community Relationships

Philemon's response to Paul's appeal would also have had a significant impact on the broader Christian community in Colossae. By embracing Onesimus as a brother, Philemon would have set an example of Christian love and forgiveness for others to follow. This example would have strengthened the community's commitment to the principles of restorative justice and mutual support.

Strengthened Bonds with Paul and Other Leaders

By responding positively to Paul's appeal, Philemon would have strengthened his bonds with Paul and other leaders in the early Christian movement. Paul's expression of confidence in Philemon's obedience and willingness to do even more than asked highlights the trust and respect that existed between them.

Confident of your obedience, I write to you, knowing that you will do even more than I ask. (Philemon 1:21)

This strengthened bond would have fostered greater unity and collaboration within the early church, enhancing its overall effectiveness and witness.

Broader Implications for the Early Christian Community

A Model for Christian Conduct

Philemon's response to Paul's appeal would have served as a model for Christian conduct within the early church. It demonstrated how believers were expected to transcend social norms, forgive one another, and embrace their new identity in Christ as members of a single spiritual family.

Promoting Unity and Inclusivity

By forgiving Onesimus and welcoming him as a brother, Philemon would have promoted unity and inclusivity within the Christian community. This act of reconciliation would have reinforced the message that in Christ, there is no longer Jew or Greek, slave or free, but all are one (Galatians 3:28). This message of unity and inclusivity was crucial for the growth and cohesion of the early church.

Strengthening the Church's Witness

The reconciliation between Philemon and Onesimus would have strengthened the church's witness to the transformative power of the gospel. It provided a tangible example of how Christian love and forgiveness could break down social barriers and create new, equitable relationships. This powerful testimony would have attracted others to the faith and demonstrated the distinctiveness of the Christian community.

Paul's appeal to Philemon had a profound impact on Philemon's life and faith. By challenging Philemon to forgive Onesimus and embrace him as a brother, Paul encouraged him to practice the core Christian virtues of love, forgiveness, and reconciliation. This process deepened Philemon's faith, strengthened his relationships, and set an example for the broader Christian community.

The transformation of Philemon's relationship with Onesimus and the broader implications for the early church highlights the power of restorative justice and the principles of the gospel to create new, transformative relationships. By understanding the impact of Paul's intervention on Philemon, we can gain valuable insights into the enduring relevance of these principles for contemporary contexts.

In the next chapter, we will explore the broader impact of Paul's intervention on the early Christian community, examining how this case of restorative justice influenced the church's teachings and practices. By understanding the communal implications, we can gain a more comprehensive view of the transformative power of restorative justice within the Christian faith.

THE BROADER IMPLICATIONS FOR THE EARLY CHURCH

Paul's letter to Philemon serves not only as a personal appeal for forgiveness and reconciliation but also as a model for the early church in handling conflicts and promoting restorative justice principles. The way Paul addresses the situation between Philemon and Onesimus provides valuable lessons for the early Christian community, influencing its teachings, practices, and overall approach to justice and relationships. This chapter explores the broader implications of Paul's letter for the early church and how it shaped the community's understanding and application of restorative justice.

A Model for Handling Conflicts

Emphasizing Personal Appeals Over Commands

One of the key aspects of Paul's approach in his letter to Philemon is his emphasis on personal appeal rather than authoritative commands. Paul, an apostle with significant authority, chooses to appeal to Philemon's sense of Christian duty and love instead of ordering him to forgive Onesimus. He writes:

Therefore, although in Christ I could be bold and order you to do what you ought to do, yet I prefer to appeal to you on the basis of love. (Philemon 1:8-9)

This approach sets a precedent for the early church in handling conflicts. It highlights the importance of addressing issues through personal engagement and appeals to shared values rather than relying solely on authority and commands. This method fosters a sense of voluntary action and mutual respect, which are crucial for genuine reconciliation.

Encouraging Voluntary and Heartfelt Responses

Paul's emphasis on voluntary action is evident throughout his letter. He wants Philemon's response to be genuine and heartfelt, arising from his convictions rather than external pressure. Paul writes:

But I did not want to do anything without your consent so any favor you do would not seem forced but would be voluntary. (Philemon 1:14)

This principle of encouraging voluntary and heartfelt responses is essential for the early church's approach to conflict resolution. It ensures that reconciliation and forgiveness are authentic, fostering deeper and more lasting relationships within the community.

Promoting Restorative Justice Principles

Restitution and Making Amends

Paul's offer to repay any debt Onesimus owes is a clear demonstration of the principle of restitution, a key component of restorative justice. By offering to take on Onesimus's debt, Paul ensures that the harm caused by Onesimus's actions is addressed and repaired:

If he has done you any wrong or owes you anything, charge it to me. I, Paul, am writing this with my own hand. I will pay it back. (Philemon 1:18-19)

This act of restitution serves as a model for the early church, emphasizing the importance of making amends and addressing the harm caused by wrongdoing. It highlights the need for offenders to take responsibility for their actions and for the community to support the process of making things right.

Focus on Relationship Restoration

Paul's primary goal in his letter is the restoration of the relationship between Philemon and Onesimus. He seeks to transform their relationship from one of master and slave to one of brothers in Christ:

Perhaps the reason he was separated from you for a little while was that you might have him back forever—no longer as a slave, but better than a slave, as a dear brother. (Philemon 1:15-16)

This focus on relationship restoration is a fundamental principle of restorative justice. It emphasizes the importance of healing and rebuilding relationships rather than simply punishing the offender. The early church adopted this approach, prioritizing reconciliation and community harmony.

Equality and Brotherhood

Paul's appeal to Philemon to receive Onesimus as a brother rather than a slave underscores the Christian principle of equality and brotherhood. In Christ, all believers are equal, regardless of their social status:

No longer as a slave, but better than a slave, as a dear brother. (Philemon 1:16)

This message of equality and brotherhood was revolutionary in the context of the Roman Empire, where social hierarchies were deeply entrenched. By promoting these principles, Paul's letter helped to shape the early church's understanding of community, where all members were to be treated with dignity and respect.

Influencing Early Church Teachings and Practices

A Blueprint for Church Discipline

Paul's handling of the situation between Philemon and Onesimus provides a blueprint for church discipline and conflict resolution. It demonstrates the importance of addressing conflicts with empathy, personal engagement, and a focus on reconciliation. This approach influenced how the early church dealt with internal conflicts, emphasizing restorative practices over punitive measures.

Shaping the Community's Identity

The principles outlined in Paul's letter contributed to shaping the early church's identity as a community committed to love, forgiveness, and mutual support. By modeling these values in their interactions, early Christians distinguished themselves from the broader society and demonstrated the transformative power of the gospel.

Strengthening the Church's Witness

The reconciliation between Philemon and Onesimus, facilitated by Paul's intervention, served as a powerful testimony to the wider society. It showcased the Christian community's commitment to justice, equality, and reconciliation. This strong witness attracted others to the faith and reinforced the church's credibility and moral authority.

Fostering a Culture of Compassion and Support

Paul's letter fosters a culture of compassion and support within the early church. By advocating for Onesimus and offering to bear the cost of restitution, Paul sets an example of sacrificial love and support. This culture encourages believers to look out for one another, provide support in times of need, and actively work toward reconciliation and restoration.

The Lasting Legacy of Paul's Letter

A Timeless Model for Restorative Justice

The principles and practices demonstrated in Paul's letter to Philemon have a timeless quality, providing a model for restorative justice that remains relevant today. The emphasis on empathy, personal engagement, restitution, and relationship restoration offers valuable lessons for contemporary conflict resolution and justice practices.

Inspiring Future Generations

Paul's letter has inspired countless generations of Christians to pursue reconciliation and restorative justice in their own lives and communities. By following Paul's example, believers are encouraged to transcend social barriers, practice radical forgiveness, and work towards building communities characterized by love, equality, and mutual respect.

Paul's letter to Philemon serves as a profound model for the early church in handling conflicts and promoting restorative justice principles. By emphasizing personal appeals, voluntary action, restitution, and relationship restoration, Paul set a precedent for how the Christian community should address wrongdoing and foster reconciliation. These principles helped shape the early church's teachings and practices, strengthening its identity and witness.

The broader implications of Paul's intervention extend beyond the immediate reconciliation between Philemon and Onesimus, offering timeless lessons for the church in every generation. By embracing these principles, the Christian community can continue to demonstrate the transformative power of the gospel and work towards justice, healing, and restoration in a broken world.

In the next chapter, we will explore the lasting impact of Paul's letter on the broader Christian community and how its principles can be applied in contemporary contexts to address conflicts and promote restorative justice in today's world.

CHAPTER 07

LESSONS FROM PHILEMON FOR MODERN RESTORATIVE JUSTICE

The principles and practices demonstrated in Paul's letter to Philemon offer timeless insights for modern restorative justice. By examining key elements such as empathy, mediation, restitution, and reconciliation, we can draw valuable lessons for contemporary applications. This chapter explores how these principles from Philemon can be effectively integrated into modern restorative justice practices to promote healing, accountability, and restored relationships.

Principles and Practices

Empathy and Compassion

Understanding the Role of Empathy

Empathy is the foundation of restorative justice. It involves understanding and sharing the feelings of another person, which is crucial for addressing harm and fostering reconciliation. In his letter to Philemon, Paul shows deep empathy for Onesimus, acknowledging his past wrongs but also recognizing his potential and new identity in Christ:

I appeal to you for my son Onesimus, who became my son while I was in chains. Formerly he was useless to you, but now he has become useful both to you and to me. (Philemon 1:10-11)

Applying Empathy in Modern Practices

Modern restorative justice practices can benefit greatly from the emphasis on empathy seen in Paul's approach. Practitioners should strive to understand the perspectives of all parties involved, including victims, offenders, and the community. This understanding fosters a compassionate environment where healing and reconciliation can occur.

Mediation and Advocacy

The Role of Mediation

Paul acts as a mediator between Philemon and Onesimus, facilitating communication and understanding. His approach highlights the importance of mediation in resolving conflicts and promoting reconciliation. Paul's mediation is marked by respect, personal investment, and a focus on voluntary action:

Therefore, although in Christ I could be bold and order you to do what you ought to do, yet I prefer to appeal to you based on love. (Philemon 1:8-9)

Modern Mediation Techniques

Modern restorative justice practices can incorporate mediation by bringing together all parties in a safe and structured environment. Trained mediators can help facilitate open and respectful dialogue, ensuring that each party's voice is heard and their concerns addressed. This process helps build trust and paves the way for mutually agreed-upon solutions.

The Importance of Advocacy

Paul's advocacy for Onesimus goes beyond mediation. He actively supports Onesimus by highlighting his transformation and offering to make restitution on his behalf. This advocacy underscores the importance of supporting individuals who seek to make amends:

If he has done you any wrong or owes you anything, charge it to me. I, Paul, am writing this with my own hand. I will pay it back. (Philemon 1:18-19)

Advocacy in Modern Contexts

In modern restorative justice, advocacy can take various forms, including legal support, counseling, and community backing. Advocates play a crucial role in ensuring that offenders have the resources and support they need to make amends and reintegrate into the community. Advocacy also involves ensuring that victims' needs are addressed and that they receive appropriate support and restitution.

Restitution and Making Amends

Paul's Offer of Restitution

Restitution is a key component of restorative justice, aiming to repair harm and restore relationships. Paul's offer to repay any debt Onesimus owes embodies this principle and demonstrates the importance of making amends:

If he has done you any wrong or owes you anything, charge it to me. I, Paul, am writing this with my own hand. I will pay it back. (Philemon 1:18-19)

Implementing Restitution Today

Modern restorative justice practices should emphasize restitution as a way to address the harm caused by wrongdoing. This can include financial compensation, community service, or other forms of reparation that directly address the needs of the victim. Restitution helps to restore trust and balance in relationships, promoting healing and closure for all parties involved.

Reconciliation and Relationship Restoration

The Goal of Reconciliation

The ultimate goal of restorative justice is to achieve reconciliation and restore relationships. Paul's appeal to Philemon to receive Onesimus as a brother rather than a slave exemplifies this goal:

Perhaps the reason he was separated from you for a little while was that you might have him back forever—no longer as a slave, but better than a slave, as a dear brother. (Philemon 1:15-16)

Reconciliation in Modern Practices

Modern restorative justice practices should prioritize reconciliation by creating opportunities for offenders and victims to rebuild their relationships. This involves facilitated dialogues, apologies, and commitments to future conduct that align with shared values and mutual respect. The focus on relationship restoration helps to create a more harmonious and cohesive community.

Practical Applications of Restorative Justice Principles

Restorative Circles

Restorative circles are a practical application of the principles outlined in Paul's letter. These circles bring together victims, offenders, and community members to discuss the impact of the offense and to develop a plan for making amends. The circle process fosters empathy, open communication, and mutual support, embodying the principles of mediation, restitution, and reconciliation.

Victim-Offender Mediation

Victim-offender mediation provides a structured setting where victims and offenders can communicate directly. This process allows victims to express their feelings and needs, while offenders have the opportunity to take responsibility for their actions and make restitution. The mediator facilitates the conversation, ensuring that it remains respectful and focused on healing and resolution.

Community Service and Restitution Programs

Programs that incorporate community service and restitution help offenders make tangible amends for their actions. These programs can be tailored to address the specific harm caused by the offense, promoting accountability and providing a way for offenders to contribute positively to their community. Such programs are integral to the restorative justice process, reinforcing the principles of making amends and restoring relationships.

Support and Reintegration Programs

Support and reintegration programs are essential for helping offenders transition back into their communities. These programs provide resources such as counseling, education, job training, and mentorship, ensuring that offenders have the support they need to succeed and avoid reoffending. Advocacy plays a crucial role in these programs, helping to navigate systemic barriers and ensure that offenders have access to necessary resources.

The principles and practices demonstrated in Paul's letter to Philemon offer valuable lessons for modern restorative justice. By emphasizing empathy, mediation, restitution, and reconciliation, Paul provides a timeless model for addressing conflicts and promoting healing and restoration. These principles can be effectively integrated into contemporary restorative justice practices, fostering accountability, healing, and stronger relationships within communities.

By applying the lessons from Philemon, modern restorative justice can create more compassionate and supportive environments, where individuals are encouraged to take responsibility for their actions, make amends, and rebuild relationships. These practices not only address the immediate harm caused by wrongdoing but also contribute to the long-term health and cohesion of communities, reflecting the transformative power of justice and reconciliation.

APPLICATION IN CONTEMPORARY SETTINGS

The lessons from Paul's letter to Philemon provide valuable insights for applying restorative justice principles in various contemporary settings. These principles can be integrated into criminal justice systems, community conflict resolution, and personal relationships, promoting healing, accountability, and reconciliation. This chapter explores how the key lessons from Philemon can be effectively applied in these different contexts.

Application in Criminal Justice

Restorative Justice Programs

Victim-Offender Mediation

Victim-offender mediation is a restorative justice practice that brings victims and offenders together to discuss the impact of the crime and to find ways to make amends. This approach aligns with Paul's method of facilitating direct communication between Philemon and Onesimus. In these programs, trained mediators help create a safe environment where both parties can express their feelings and needs, fostering empathy and understanding.

- Case Example: A juvenile offender who has committed theft meets with the victim. Through mediation, the offender understands the emotional and financial impact of their actions, apologizes, and agrees to work for the victim to repay the loss.

Restitution and Community Service

Restitution programs require offenders to compensate victims for their losses, while community service programs involve offenders contributing positively to their communities. Paul's offer to repay Onesimus's debt is a clear example of restitution, demonstrating the importance of making amends.

- Case Example: A person convicted of vandalism participates in community service by cleaning and repairing damaged public property, directly addressing the harm caused and contributing to community well-being.

Rehabilitation and Reintegration

Supportive Reintegration Programs

Rehabilitation and reintegration programs provide offenders with the support they need to successfully reenter society. These programs often include counseling, job training, education, and mentorship, reflecting Paul's advocacy and support for Onesimus.

- Case Example: A recently released inmate joins a reintegration program that offers job training and counseling.

With the support of mentors, the individual finds stable employment and avoids reoffending.

Advocacy for Offenders

Advocates play a crucial role in helping offenders navigate the challenges of reintegration, much like Paul advocated for Onesimus. Advocates can provide legal assistance, connect offenders with resources, and offer emotional support.

- Case Example: An advocacy organization helps former inmates secure housing, find employment, and access mental health services, reducing recidivism and supporting their transition back into the community.

Application in Community Conflicts

Restorative Circles

Facilitating Dialogue and Understanding

Restorative circles bring together those involved in a conflict, including victims, offenders, and community members. These circles facilitate open dialogue and understanding, promoting reconciliation and healing, similar to how Paul facilitated reconciliation between Philemon and Onesimus.

- Case Example: In a neighborhood dispute over noise complaints, a restorative circle allows residents to express their concerns, listen to each other, and agree on solutions that foster mutual respect and community harmony.

Building Community Cohesion

Restorative circles also strengthen community cohesion by addressing underlying issues and promoting collective responsibility. This approach helps build stronger, more resilient communities.

- Case Example: In a school setting, a restorative circle addresses bullying by involving students, teachers, and parents. Together, they develop strategies to create a safer and more supportive school environment.

Mediation Services

Resolving Disputes Amicably

Community mediation services provide a neutral platform for resolving disputes amicably. These services align with Paul's approach of mediation, focusing on voluntary participation and mutual agreement.

- Case Example: In a dispute between business partners, a mediator helps facilitate a discussion where both parties express their grievances and work towards a fair resolution, preserving their professional relationship.

Empowering Parties to Find Solutions

Mediation empowers parties to find their own solutions, ensuring that outcomes are mutually satisfactory and sustainable.

- Case Example: A mediation session between neighbors in a property boundary dispute results in a mutually agreed-upon solution that respects both parties' needs and strengthens their relationship.

Application in Personal Relationships

Conflict Resolution in Families

Promoting Forgiveness and Reconciliation

Paul's emphasis on forgiveness and reconciliation in his letter to Philemon provides a model for resolving family conflicts. By promoting empathy, understanding, and voluntary forgiveness, family members can rebuild trust and strengthen their relationships.

- Case Example: In a family conflict over inheritance, a facilitated conversation helps family members express their feelings, understand each other's perspectives, and agree on a fair distribution, promoting healing and unity.

Supporting Personal Growth and Transformation

Encouraging personal growth and transformation, as Paul did with Onesimus, can help family members overcome past grievances and build healthier relationships.

- Case Example: A parent supports their adult child's efforts to overcome past mistakes by providing emotional support and encouraging positive changes, fostering a renewed and stronger relationship.

Restorative Practices in Friendships

Addressing Harm and Making Amends

In friendships, restorative practices can help address harm and make amends, promoting healing and deeper connections.

- Case Example: After a breach of trust, friends engage in a restorative dialogue where the offending party acknowledges their actions, apologizes, and makes efforts to restore trust, leading to reconciliation.

Strengthening Bonds through Empathy

Practicing empathy, as Paul demonstrated, can strengthen bonds in friendships by fostering a deeper understanding and connection.

- Case Example: Friends navigate a misunderstanding by actively listening to each other's perspectives, validating feelings, and finding common ground, resulting in a stronger, more empathetic relationship.

The lessons from Paul's letter to Philemon offer valuable insights for applying restorative justice principles in contemporary settings. By emphasizing empathy, mediation, restitution, and reconciliation, these principles can be effectively integrated into criminal justice systems, community conflict resolution, and personal relationships.

In criminal justice, these principles promote healing, accountability, and successful reintegration of offenders. In community conflicts, they foster dialogue, understanding, and stronger community cohesion. In personal relationships, they encourage forgiveness, personal growth, and deeper connections.

By drawing on the timeless wisdom of Paul's letter, modern restorative justice practices can create more compassionate, supportive, and harmonious environments, reflecting the transformative power of justice and reconciliation.

CHALLENGES AND OPPORTUNITIES

Implementing restorative justice principles in contemporary society presents both significant challenges and substantial opportunities. While the process of incorporating these principles can be complex and demanding, the potential for healing, transformation, and strengthened communities makes it a worthwhile endeavor. This chapter explores the key challenges faced in applying restorative justice principles and the opportunities they offer for fostering a more just and compassionate society.

Challenges in Implementing Restorative Justice

Institutional Resistance

Entrenched Systems of Retributive Justice

One of the primary challenges in implementing restorative justice is the deep entrenchment of retributive justice systems. Many legal and correctional institutions are built around the idea of punishment and deterrence rather than restoration and reconciliation. Shifting these institutions towards a restorative approach requires significant changes in policy, practice, and mindset.

- Example: Traditional court systems focus on determining guilt and administering punishment, often leaving little room for victim-offender dialogue or community involvement.

Lack of Awareness and Understanding

Another challenge is the lack of awareness and understanding of restorative justice principles among practitioners, policymakers, and the general public. Misconceptions about restorative justice being too lenient or ineffective can hinder its adoption and implementation.

- Example: Misunderstanding restorative justice as merely an alternative to punishment rather than a comprehensive approach to addressing harm and fostering healing.

Resource Constraints

Funding and Staffing

Implementing restorative justice programs often requires additional resources, including funding and staffing. These programs necessitate trained mediators, facilitators, and support staff to effectively manage restorative processes.

- Example: Community-based restorative justice programs may struggle to secure funding for hiring and training staff, limiting their capacity to serve.

Infrastructure and Support Systems

Adequate infrastructure and support systems are essential for restorative justice programs to succeed. This includes facilities for meetings, access to counseling and support services, and administrative support.

- Example: Lack of appropriate spaces for holding restorative circles or victim-offender dialogues can impede the implementation of restorative practices.

Cultural and Societal Barriers

Social Norms and Attitudes

Cultural and societal norms that emphasize punishment and retribution over reconciliation and healing can be significant barriers to implementing restorative justice.

Changing these deeply ingrained attitudes requires comprehensive education and advocacy efforts.

- Example: Societal beliefs that equate justice with punishment may resist the idea of restorative justice, viewing it as insufficiently punitive.

Diverse Needs and Perspectives

Restorative justice processes must be adaptable to the diverse needs and perspectives of individuals and communities. This diversity can present challenges in designing and implementing programs that are inclusive and effective for all participants.

- Example: Cultural differences in communication styles and conflict resolution approaches can complicate the facilitation of restorative justice processes.

Opportunities for Healing and Transformation

Enhancing Victim Healing and Empowerment

Providing a Voice for Victims

Restorative justice offers victims a platform to express their feelings, needs, and perspectives, which can be a crucial part of the healing process. By participating in restorative processes, victims gain a sense of empowerment and closure that is often lacking in traditional justice systems.

- Example: Victims of theft participating in restorative dialogues can share the emotional and practical impact of the crime, leading to a more meaningful resolution.

Tailored Restitution and Support

Restorative justice allows for tailored restitution that directly addresses the harm experienced by victims. This personalized approach can lead to more satisfactory and effective outcomes for victims.

- Example: An offender providing community service in a way that directly benefits the victim, such as repairing damage caused by the offense.

Promoting Offender Accountability and Rehabilitation

Encouraging Personal Responsibility

Restorative justice emphasizes personal responsibility and accountability, encouraging offenders to acknowledge their actions and make amends. This approach can lead to genuine remorse and a commitment to change.

- Example: An offender participating in a restorative circle may develop a deeper understanding of the impact of their actions and commit to personal growth and positive behavior changes.

Supporting Rehabilitation and Reintegration

Restorative justice programs often include support for rehabilitation and reintegration, helping offenders build skills and access resources necessary for successful reentry into society. This holistic approach reduces recidivism and promotes long-term positive outcomes.

- Example: A restorative justice program that combines dialogue with educational and vocational training, supporting offenders in building a stable and productive future.

Strengthening Community Bonds

Fostering Collective Responsibility

Restorative justice emphasizes the role of the community in addressing harm and fostering healing. By involving community members in restorative processes, these programs promote collective responsibility and strengthen social bonds.

- Example: Community members participating in restorative circles to address neighborhood conflicts, leading to a more cohesive and supportive community environment.

Building Trust and Social Capital

Restorative justice processes build trust and social capital within communities by demonstrating a commitment to fairness, empathy, and mutual respect. These strengthened relationships create a foundation for more resilient and harmonious communities.

- Example: A community that regularly engages in restorative practices may experience increased trust and cooperation among its members, reducing the likelihood of future conflicts.

Advancing a More Compassionate Justice System

Shifting the Focus from Punishment to Healing

Restorative justice offers an alternative vision of justice that prioritizes healing over punishment. By focusing on repairing harm and restoring relationships, restorative justice aligns more closely with values of compassion and humanity.

- Example: A justice system that incorporates restorative practices may see lower rates of recidivism and higher levels of satisfaction among victims and offenders, reflecting a more compassionate approach to justice.

Creating Sustainable and Just Outcomes

Restorative justice seeks sustainable and just outcomes by addressing the root causes of harm and involving all stakeholders in the resolution process. This comprehensive approach leads to more durable and equitable resolutions.

- Example: A restorative justice program that addresses underlying issues such as poverty, addiction, or mental health challenges, creating conditions for long-term positive change.

While implementing restorative justice principles presents significant challenges, the opportunities they offer for healing and transformation are profound. By addressing institutional resistance, resource constraints, and cultural barriers, restorative justice can create more compassionate and effective approaches to addressing harm and fostering reconciliation.

The principles of empathy, mediation, restitution, and reconciliation demonstrated in Paul's letter to Philemon provide a timeless model for contemporary restorative justice practices. By applying these principles in criminal justice systems, community conflict resolution, and personal relationships, we can promote healing, accountability, and stronger communities.

Ultimately, the successful implementation of restorative justice requires a commitment to change, education, and advocacy. By embracing these principles and addressing the challenges, we can build a more just and compassionate society, reflecting the transformative power of restorative justice.

CHAPTER 08

CONCLUSION

Summary of Key Points

The Book of Philemon, though brief, provides a profound illustration of the principles and power of restorative justice. By examining Paul's letter to Philemon, we can glean valuable insights into how restorative justice can transform relationships and promote reconciliation. This chapter summarizes the key points explored throughout this book and reflects on the enduring relevance of these principles for contemporary society.

The Power of Restorative Justice

Paul's letter to Philemon serves as a powerful example of restorative justice in action. Through his appeal, Paul demonstrates how empathy, mediation, restitution, and reconciliation can address harm, heal relationships, and foster a more just and compassionate community. The transformative power of restorative justice lies in its ability to promote understanding, accountability, and healing for all parties involved.

Key Principles of Restorative Justice

Empathy and Compassion

Paul's deep empathy for Onesimus and his appeal to Philemon's sense of love and compassion underscore the importance of empathy in restorative justice. By understanding and sharing the feelings of others, we can create an environment conducive to healing and reconciliation.

Mediation and Advocacy

Paul's role as a mediator and advocate highlights the importance of facilitating communication and supporting those involved in conflicts. Mediation helps bridge gaps and foster understanding, while advocacy ensures that individuals have the support and resources needed to make amends and rebuild relationships.

Restitution and Making Amends

Restitution is a critical component of restorative justice, as demonstrated by Paul's offer to repay any debt Onesimus owes. Making amends addresses the harm caused and helps restore balance and trust in relationships. Restitution emphasizes accountability and the need to repair the damage done by wrongful actions.

Reconciliation and Relationship Restoration

The ultimate goal of restorative justice is to achieve reconciliation and restore relationships. Paul's appeal for Philemon to receive Onesimus as a brother in Christ exemplifies this goal. Reconciliation involves forgiveness, rebuilding trust, and fostering a renewed sense of mutual respect and love.

Challenges and Opportunities

Implementing restorative justice principles in contemporary settings presents both challenges and opportunities. Overcoming institutional resistance, resource constraints, and cultural barriers requires significant effort and commitment. However, the opportunities for healing, transformation, and strengthened communities make these efforts worthwhile.

Enhancing Victim Healing and Empowerment

Restorative justice provides victims with a voice and a platform to express their needs and perspectives, fostering healing and empowerment. By addressing the harm experienced by victims, restorative justice promotes a sense of closure and validation.

Promoting Offender Accountability and Rehabilitation

Restorative justice encourages offenders to take responsibility for their actions and make amends. This approach fosters genuine remorse and a commitment to change, supporting rehabilitation and successful reintegration into society.

Strengthening Community Bonds

By involving community members in restorative processes, restorative justice fosters collective responsibility and strengthens social bonds. This approach promotes trust, cooperation, and a sense of shared responsibility for maintaining justice and harmony.

Enduring Relevance for Contemporary Society

The principles and practices demonstrated in the Book of Philemon have enduring relevance for contemporary society. By applying these lessons in various settings, including criminal justice, community conflict resolution, and personal relationships, we can create more compassionate and effective approaches to addressing harm and fostering reconciliation.

Application in Criminal Justice

Restorative justice practices such as victim-offender mediation, restitution programs, and support for rehabilitation and reintegration offer meaningful alternatives to traditional punitive approaches. These practices promote healing, accountability, and successful reentry into society.

Application in Community Conflicts

Restorative circles and mediation services provide effective tools for resolving community conflicts. These practices foster dialogue, understanding, and stronger community cohesion, addressing underlying issues and promoting collective responsibility.

Application in Personal Relationships

In personal relationships, restorative justice principles encourage forgiveness, personal growth, and deeper connections. By addressing harm and making amends, individuals can rebuild trust and strengthen their bonds.

The Book of Philemon illustrates the transformative power of restorative justice in addressing harm, healing relationships, and fostering reconciliation. By emphasizing empathy, mediation, restitution, and reconciliation, Paul provides a timeless model for promoting justice and compassion in our interactions with others.

As we seek to apply these principles in contemporary society, we face both challenges and opportunities. Overcoming obstacles requires commitment, education, and advocacy, but the potential for healing and transformation makes these efforts profoundly worthwhile. By embracing restorative justice, we can build more just, compassionate, and harmonious communities, reflecting the enduring wisdom and transformative power of the gospel.

THE LASTING LEGACY OF PAUL'S APPROACH

Paul's approach in his letter to Philemon has left a lasting legacy for the church and provides valuable insights for contemporary justice practices. By emphasizing principles of restorative justice such as empathy, mediation, restitution, and reconciliation, Paul set a precedent for addressing conflicts and fostering healing in ways that remain relevant today. This chapter explores the enduring impact of Paul's approach and its implications for modern justice systems and community practices.

The Legacy of the Church

A Model for Christian Conduct

Paul's handling of the situation between Philemon and Onesimus offers a timeless model for Christian conduct. It demonstrates how believers are called to practice forgiveness, love, and reconciliation in their relationships. This model has shaped Christian teachings and practices for centuries, influencing how the church addresses internal conflicts and promotes community harmony.

Emphasizing Forgiveness and Reconciliation

Paul's letter underscores the importance of forgiveness and reconciliation as core Christian values. By urging Philemon to forgive Onesimus and embrace him as a brother, Paul highlights the transformative power of the gospel in healing relationships and restoring community.

Perhaps the reason he was separated from you for a little while was that you might have him back forever—no longer as a slave, but better than a slave, as a dear brother. (Philemon 1:15-16)

Strengthening Church Unity

The principles demonstrated in Paul's letter have also contributed to strengthening church unity. By promoting equality and mutual respect, Paul's approach encourages believers to see each other as members of one spiritual family, regardless of social status or past transgressions. This emphasis on unity has helped foster a sense of belonging and solidarity within the church.

Breaking Down Social Barriers

Paul's appeal to Philemon to receive Onesimus as a brother challenges existing social hierarchies and promotes a vision of the church as an inclusive and egalitarian community. This message of unity and inclusivity continues to inspire efforts to break down social barriers and promote justice and equality within the church and beyond.

Insights for Contemporary Justice Practices

Addressing Institutional Resistance

Paul's approach provides valuable insights for addressing institutional resistance to restorative justice. By appealing to shared values and emphasizing the benefits of reconciliation, Paul demonstrates how to navigate resistance and promote restorative practices within existing structures.

Building on Shared Values

In contemporary settings, restorative justice advocates can draw on shared community values to promote the benefits of restorative practices. By highlighting the alignment between restorative justice principles and broader societal values of fairness, empathy, and community well-being, advocates can build support for these practices.

Overcoming Resource Constraints

Paul's investment in Onesimus's case illustrates the importance of resourcefulness and commitment in overcoming resource constraints. Modern restorative justice programs can benefit from partnerships, community involvement, and innovative approaches to securing funding and support.

Leveraging Community Resources

Restorative justice programs can leverage community resources, including volunteer mediators, local organizations, and partnerships with businesses and educational institutions. By building a network of support, these programs can overcome resource limitations and expand their reach.

Promoting Cultural Change

Paul's letter exemplifies the potential for cultural change through advocacy and personal example. By living out the principles of restorative justice, Paul sets a powerful example for others to follow. Contemporary practitioners can similarly promote cultural change by embodying restorative values and demonstrating their effectiveness.

Education and Advocacy

Education and advocacy are critical for shifting cultural attitudes toward restorative justice. By raising awareness, providing training, and sharing success stories, practitioners can build a broader understanding and acceptance of restorative practices.

Enhancing Victim and Offender Support

Paul's compassionate approach to both Philemon and Onesimus highlights the importance of supporting both victims and offenders in the restorative process. Modern practices can draw on this insight to provide comprehensive support that addresses the needs of all parties involved.

Holistic Support Services

Restorative justice programs should offer holistic support services, including counseling, legal assistance, and practical help for both victims and offenders. By addressing the full range of needs, these programs can promote healing and successful reintegration.

Encouraging Personal Responsibility

Paul's emphasis on personal responsibility and restitution underscores the importance of accountability in restorative justice. Contemporary practices can build on this principle by encouraging offenders to take responsibility for their actions and make amends.

Structured Accountability Processes

Structured accountability processes, such as restorative circles and victim-offender mediation, provide frameworks for offenders to acknowledge their actions and develop plans for restitution. These processes promote genuine accountability and facilitate meaningful amends.

Fostering Community Involvement

Paul's approach demonstrates the value of involving the community in the restorative process. Modern practices can enhance their effectiveness by fostering community involvement and collective responsibility.

Community-Based Restorative Justice

Community-based restorative justice programs engage local residents in addressing conflicts and promoting healing. By involving the community, these programs build social capital and strengthen community bonds.

Paul's approach in his letter to Philemon leaves a lasting legacy for the church and offers valuable insights for contemporary justice practices. By emphasizing empathy, mediation, restitution, and reconciliation, Paul set a powerful precedent for addressing conflicts and fostering healing. These principles continue to inspire and inform modern restorative justice programs, promoting more compassionate and effective approaches to justice.

As we seek to apply these principles in contemporary settings, we face both challenges and opportunities. Overcoming obstacles requires commitment, education, and advocacy, but the potential for healing and transformation makes these efforts profoundly worthwhile. By embracing restorative justice, we can build more just, compassionate, and harmonious communities, reflecting the enduring wisdom and transformative power of Paul's approach.

ENCOURAGEMENT FOR CONTINUED PRACTICE OF RESTORATIVE JUSTICE

The principles of restorative justice, as demonstrated in Paul's letter to Philemon, provide a powerful framework for addressing harm and fostering reconciliation in contemporary society. Believers are encouraged to continue practicing these principles, embodying empathy, reconciliation, and restitution in their lives and communities.

This chapter offers encouragement and practical guidance for sustaining and expanding the practice of restorative justice.

Embracing Empathy

The Foundation of Empathy

Empathy is the cornerstone of restorative justice. It involves understanding and sharing the feelings of others, which is essential for addressing harm and promoting healing. Paul's deep empathy for Onesimus and his appeal to Philemon's compassion serve as a model for how empathy can transform relationships.

I appeal to you for my son Onesimus, who became my son while I was in chains. Formerly he was useless to you, but now he has become useful both to you and to me. (Philemon 1:10-11)

Cultivating Empathy in Daily Life

Believers are encouraged to cultivate empathy in their daily interactions. This involves actively listening to others, seeking to understand their perspectives, and responding with compassion and kindness. By practicing empathy, individuals can create a more supportive and understanding community.

Practical Steps to Cultivate Empathy

- Active Listening: Pay close attention to what others are saying without interrupting. Show that you value their perspective.

- Reflective Responses: Reflect back what you hear, showing that you understand and empathize with their feelings.

- Putting Yourself in Others' Shoes: Try to imagine how you would feel if you were in the other person's situation.

Pursuing Reconciliation

The Goal of Reconciliation

Reconciliation is at the heart of restorative justice. It involves healing relationships, rebuilding trust, and fostering mutual respect and understanding. Paul's call for Philemon to receive Onesimus as a brother exemplifies the transformative power of reconciliation.

Perhaps the reason he was separated from you for a little while was that you might have him back forever—no longer as a slave, but better than a slave, as a dear brother. (Philemon 1:15-16)

Fostering Reconciliation in Communities

Believers are encouraged to actively pursue reconciliation in their communities. This involves addressing conflicts, facilitating dialogue, and promoting forgiveness and mutual respect. By fostering reconciliation, individuals can help build stronger, more cohesive communities.

Practical Steps to Foster Reconciliation

- Facilitate Dialogue: Create opportunities for open and respectful communication between parties in conflict.

- Promote Forgiveness: Encourage individuals to forgive past wrongs and seek to understand each other's perspectives.

- Build Trust: Work to rebuild trust through consistent, trustworthy behavior and by fulfilling commitments.

Practicing Restitution

The Importance of Making Amends

Restitution is a key component of restorative justice, emphasizing the need to make amends for harm caused. Paul's offer to repay any debt Onesimus owes highlights the importance of addressing harm and taking responsibility for one's actions.

If he has done you any wrong or owes you anything, charge it to me. I, Paul, am writing this with my own hand. I will pay it back. (Philemon 1:18-19)

Implementing Restitution in Everyday Life

Believers are encouraged to practice restitution by making amends for any harm they have caused. This involves acknowledging wrongdoing, offering sincere apologies, and taking concrete steps to repair the damage. By practicing restitution, individuals demonstrate accountability and contribute to the healing process.

Practical Steps to Practice Restitution

- Acknowledge Wrongdoing: Honestly acknowledge the harm you have caused and take responsibility for your actions.

- Offer Sincere Apologies: Apologize sincerely and without excuses, expressing genuine remorse for the harm done.

- Take Concrete Steps: Identify and take specific actions to repair the harm, whether through financial compensation, acts of service, or other means.

Sustaining and Expanding Restorative Justice Practices

Building a Supportive Community

To sustain and expand restorative justice practices, it is essential to build a supportive community. This involves educating others about the principles and benefits of restorative justice, creating networks of support, and advocating for systemic change.

Practical Steps to Build a Supportive Community

- Education and Awareness: Organize workshops, seminars, and discussions to educate others about restorative justice principles and practices.

- Network Building: Connect with like-minded individuals and organizations to create a network of support for restorative justice initiatives.

- Advocacy: Advocate for the inclusion of restorative justice practices in schools, workplaces, and the criminal justice system.

Leading by Example

Believers are encouraged to lead by example, demonstrating the principles of restorative justice in their own lives. By embodying empathy, reconciliation, and restitution, individuals can inspire others to adopt these practices and contribute to a culture of justice and compassion.

Practical Steps to Lead by Example

- Model Empathy: Show empathy in your interactions with others, demonstrating compassion and understanding.

- Promote Reconciliation: Actively seek to resolve conflicts and promote reconciliation in your relationships and community.

- Practice Restitution: Take responsibility for your actions and make amends for any harm you have caused.

The principles of restorative justice, as illustrated in Paul's letter to Philemon, offer a powerful framework for addressing harm and fostering healing and reconciliation. Believers are encouraged to continue practicing these principles, embodying empathy, reconciliation, and restitution in their lives and communities.

By embracing restorative justice, individuals can contribute to a more just, compassionate, and harmonious society. This ongoing commitment to restorative practices reflects the transformative power of the gospel and the enduring wisdom of Paul's approach. Through education, advocacy, and personal example, believers can sustain and expand the practice of restorative justice, creating a lasting legacy of healing and reconciliation in contemporary society.

STUDY QUESTIONS FOR EACH CHAPTER

Chapter 1: Introduction

1. How does restorative justice differ from retributive justice?

2. What are the key elements of restorative justice as described in this chapter?

3. Why is reconciliation an important goal in restorative justice?

Chapter 2: The Context of Philemon

1. What was the social and cultural background of Philemon, Onesimus, and Paul?

2. How did the Roman institution of slavery impact the relationship between Philemon and Onesimus?

3. What role did Paul play in the early Christian community, and how did this influence his letter to Philemon?

Chapter 3: Restorative Justice in the Early Church

1. How did early Christians view justice and reconciliation?

2. What examples of restorative justice can be found in the teachings of Jesus?

3. How did Paul's approach to restorative justice reflect the values of the early church?

Chapter 4: The Appeal of Paul

1. How does Paul use commendation, appeal, and personal commitment in his letter to Philemon?

2. What strategies does Paul employ to persuade Philemon to forgive Onesimus?

3. How does Paul balance authority and love in his appeal?

Chapter 5: Restitution and Restoration

1. Why is restitution an important component of restorative justice?

2. How does Paul's offer to repay Onesimus's debt illustrate the principle of making amends?

3. What impact does restitution have on the reconciliation process?

Chapter 6: The Outcome of Paul's Intervention

1. How did Paul's intervention transform Onesimus's status and relationship with Philemon?

2. What were the broader implications of this reconciliation for the early Christian community?

3. How does the transformation of Onesimus serve as a model for modern restorative justice?

Chapter 7: Challenges and Opportunities

1. What are the main challenges in implementing restorative justice in contemporary society?

2. How can these challenges be addressed to promote healing and transformation?

3. What opportunities does restorative justice offer for victims, offenders, and communities?

Chapter 8: Encouragement for Continued Practice of Restorative Justice

1. Why is it important for believers to continue practicing restorative justice?

2. How can individuals embody the principles of empathy, reconciliation, and restitution in their daily lives?

3. What steps can communities take to sustain and expand restorative justice practices?

Discussion Guides for Small Groups

Discussion Guide for Chapter 1: Introduction

- Opening Question: What are your initial thoughts on restorative justice? How does it compare to traditional views of justice you are familiar with?

- Discussion Activity: In pairs, discuss an example of a conflict you know of (personal, historical, or fictional) and how a restorative justice approach could be applied.

- Reflection: Share insights from your discussion with the larger group. What are the potential benefits and challenges of applying restorative justice to these conflicts?

Discussion Guide for Chapter 2: The Context of Philemon

- Opening Question: How does understanding the historical and cultural context of Philemon enhance our reading of Paul's letter?

- Discussion Activity: Divide into small groups to research and present on different aspects of Roman slavery and early Christian communities.

- Reflection: How did the social norms of the time influence Paul's approach, and how does this understanding affect our interpretation of his letter?

Discussion Guide for Chapter 3: Restorative Justice in the Early Church

- Opening Question: What examples of restorative justice in the New Testament resonate most with you, and why?

- Discussion Activity: Examine a New Testament story (e.g., the prodigal son, the adulterous woman) and identify elements of restorative justice.

- Reflection: How can these examples guide our current practices of justice and reconciliation in our communities?

Discussion Guide for Chapter 4: The Appeal of Paul

- Opening Question: How does Paul's tone and approach in his letter to Philemon reflect the principles of restorative justice?

- Discussion Activity: Role-play a scenario where one person must persuade another to forgive and reconcile, using Paul's techniques.

- Reflection: What strategies were most effective in your role-play, and how can they be applied in real-life situations?

Discussion Guide for Chapter 5: Restitution and Restoration

- Opening Question: Why is making amends a critical step in the process of reconciliation?

- Discussion Activity: Brainstorm different forms of restitution that can be applied in various conflict situations (e.g., personal disputes, community issues).

- Reflection: Share your ideas with the group and discuss how these forms of restitution can promote healing and trust.

Discussion Guide for Chapter 6: The Outcome of Paul's Intervention

- Opening Question: What impact did Paul's intervention have on Onesimus and Philemon, and what can we learn from this outcome?

- Discussion Activity: Create a case study based on Paul's intervention and discuss how a similar approach can be used in a modern context.

- Reflection: How can the principles of Paul's intervention be adapted to address contemporary conflicts?

Discussion Guide for Chapter 7: Challenges and Opportunities

- Opening Question: What are the biggest challenges you see in implementing restorative justice, and how might they be overcome?

- Discussion Activity: Identify a specific challenge related to restorative justice and work in groups to develop practical solutions or strategies to address it.

- Reflection: Present your solutions to the larger group and discuss the potential impact and feasibility of these strategies.

Discussion Guide for Chapter 8: Encouragement for Continued Practice of Restorative Justice

- Opening Question: How can you incorporate the principles of restorative justice into your own life and community?

- Discussion Activity: Develop an action plan for promoting restorative justice within your community, including specific steps and goals.

- Reflection: Share your action plans and commit to taking at least one step towards promoting restorative justice in the coming weeks.

Additional Resources on Restorative Justice

Books

1. "The Little Book of Restorative Justice" by Howard Zehr: A foundational text that provides a comprehensive overview of restorative justice principles and practices.

2. "Restoring Justice: An Introduction to Restorative Justice" by Daniel W. Van Ness and Karen Heetderks Strong:

An in-depth exploration of restorative justice theory and application.

3. "The New Jim Crow: Mass Incarceration in the Age of Colorblindness" by Michelle Alexander: A critical look at the criminal justice system and the need for restorative approaches.

Articles and Papers

1. "Restorative Justice: The Evidence" by Lawrence W. Sherman and Heather Strang: An evidence-based analysis of the effectiveness of restorative justice practices.

2. "Restorative Justice: An Overview" by Gerry Johnstone: A concise summary of the key concepts and debates within the field of restorative justice.

Online Resources

1. Restorative Justice Online (RJ Online): An extensive collection of articles, case studies, and resources on restorative justice (www.restorativejustice.org).

2. The Centre for Justice and Reconciliation: Offers a range of resources, including guides, training materials, and research on restorative justice (www.pfi.org/what-we-do/restore/).

Organizations

1. The International Institute for Restorative Practices (IIRP): An organization dedicated to education, research, and development of restorative practices worldwide (www.iirp.edu).

2. Restorative Justice Council (RJC): A UK-based organization that provides resources, standards, and support for restorative justice practitioners (www.restorativejustice.org.uk).

Training and Workshops

1. Restorative Practices Training: Offered by various organizations and institutions, these workshops provide hands-on training in restorative justice techniques.

2. Webinars and Online Courses: Many organizations offer online learning opportunities to gain a deeper understanding of restorative justice principles and applications.

By engaging with these resources and continuing to practice restorative justice principles, believers can contribute to creating more compassionate, just, and reconciled communities.

REFERENCES

Primary Sources

- The Holy Bible, New International Version (NIV)

Commentaries on Philemon

- Dunn, James D.G. The Epistles to the Colossians and to Philemon: A Commentary on the Greek Text. Wm. B. Eerdmans Publishing Co., 1996.

- O'Brien, Peter T. Colossians, Philemon: Word Biblical Commentary. Zondervan, 1982.

- Wright, N.T. Colossians and Philemon: An Introduction and Commentary. InterVarsity Press, 1986.

Books on Restorative Justice and Biblical Reconciliation

- Alexander, Michelle. The New Jim Crow: Mass Incarceration in the Age of Colorblindness. The New Press, 2010.

- Johnstone, Gerry. Restorative Justice: Ideas, Values, Debates. Routledge, 2011.

- Van Ness, Daniel W., and Karen Heetderks Strong. Restoring Justice: An Introduction to Restorative Justice. Routledge, 2014.

- Zehr, Howard. The Little Book of Restorative Justice. Good Books, 2015.

Articles and Papers on Restorative Justice

- Sherman, Lawrence W., and Heather Strang. "Restorative Justice: The Evidence." The Smith Institute, 2007.

- Johnstone, Gerry. "Restorative Justice: An Overview." Restorative Justice: An International Journal, vol. 1, no. 1, 2013, pp. 28-38.

Online Resources

- Restorative Justice Online (RJ Online). www.restorativejustice.org

- The Centre for Justice and Reconciliation. www.pfi.org/what-we-do/restore/

- The International Institute for Restorative Practices (IIRP). www.iirp.edu

- Restorative Justice Council (RJC). www.restorativejustice.org.uk

Additional Resources

- The Holy Bible, English Standard Version (ESV)

- Lightfoot, J.B. St. Paul's Epistles to the Colossians and to Philemon. Zondervan, 1982.

- Barclay, William. The Letters to the Philippians, Colossians, and Thessalonians. Westminster John Knox Press, 2003.

By engaging with these references, readers can deepen their understanding of the principles and practices of restorative justice and their biblical foundations. These resources offer a comprehensive guide to applying restorative justice in various contexts, promoting healing, reconciliation, and justice in contemporary society.

www.ingramcontent.com/pod-product-compliance
Lightning Source LLC
Chambersburg PA
CBHW071940150726

47999CB00001B/267